LISTENING TO THE BIBLE

A

LISTENING TO THE BIBLE

James Martin

THE SAINT ANDREW PRESS
EDINBURGH

First published in 1983 by
THE SAINT ANDREW PRESS
121 George Street, Edinburgh

Copyright © James Martin, 1983

ISBN 0 7152 0546 3

Printed in Great Britain by The Allen Lithographic Company *Kirkcaldy*

CONTENTS

INTRODUCTION

THE CHANGED SITUATION

A much-told story relates how Sir Walter Scott, drawing near to death, asked his son-in-law, Lockhart, if he would read to him.

"Read to me from the book," he said.

"The book?" asked Lockhart. "Which book?"

"*The* book," replied the dying man. "There is but one."

There was a time, and not so very long ago, when Sir Walter's estimate of the uniqueness of the Bible would have been pretty generally agreed; and agreed almost as readily by non-Christians as by Christians. The Bible was supreme among books and its supremacy was plain to all.

Times, however, have changed, and so also have attitudes towards the Bible. Today there would be great reluctance in many quarters, Christian as well as non-Christian, to subscribe unreservedly to the rating Scott awarded it.

There can, of course, be no denying that the Bible is a remarkable book. But is it not now something of a museum-piece, whose glories belong to the past?

No book, it is true, has ever been so influential upon human thought and upon human life as the Bible. And this was the case over a long period of time. Today, however, serious doubts are being aired about the Bible's right to the position it has so long occupied, and searching questions are being asked regarding its rightful place, if any, in man's future.

The question is sometimes asked as to whether or not there is any merited place even now for the Bible as a factor to influence man's thinking and living. This question ought to be taken seriously and faced honestly.

Let me put it this way. For centuries the Bible has spoken to all Christians, and to not a few non-Christians, with a trumpet-like voice of authority. But many changes have occurred and many questions are now being posed. This book attempts to deal with some of these questions.

1

IS ANYONE LISTENING?

Perhaps it is superfluous to be considering any questions about the Bible. It may be that scarcely anyone is, in any event, listening to what it has to say. That at least is the opinion many people hold.

There is no doubt that in the past the Bible spoke loudly and clearly, and whether or not they obeyed, or even agreed, practically everyone listened. The Bible indeed has had a unique history in the world of books. No more than a superficial glance at that history is enough to confirm this.

1. It is illustrated, for instance, by the way in which the text of its various component parts has been preserved with a standard of purity that no other book of ancient times comes near.

We do not, of course, possess the original manuscript, the autograph copy, of any part of the Bible writings. But that is not a matter which should occasion any surprise, for we do not possess the originals of any ancient book.

There were, after all, no printing presses in those days. Every book had to be written out by hand and every copy of it had to be manufactured in the same laborious way. This meant that in every instance there was only one "first edition" copy of a book and meant also that every subsequent copy was prepared singly.

Nowadays things are much different. When a book is published today the printing presses see to it that the first edition consists of many more than a single copy. It is worth noting that, despite this, it is often difficult, and sometimes impossible, to lay hands on first edition copies of books, even of popular and famous books, that were written in comparatively recent times. When we think of that and also of how books continued, for more than fourteen centuries after the time of Jesus, to be individual productions, written and copied entirely by hand, and when we think at the same time of the inevitable wear and tear through generations, we should not be in the least surprised that none of the original manuscripts of the scriptures has survived. It would have been most extraordinary if any of them had.

It is, however, almost as extraordinary that we possess – as beyond doubt we do – the Biblical text in a form very close to the original. Of no other piece of ancient writing can the same be said; and the exceptional purity of text with which the Bible has come to us along such a long lane of time is one of the marks of its uniqueness.

In those past days of which we speak, errors were an inevitable consequence of the method by which books were propagated. As we may well know from our own experience, no copyist of the present day is likely to prove completely accurate, no matter how painstakingly careful he may be. In ancient times the likelihood of the copyist making slips was greatly increased by the presence of a number of difficulties with which a present day copyist would not have to contend. Lighting was poor and pens were inferior. In addition, there was no punctuation and there were no space divisions between words, verses and chapters. The result was that no book of those days ever succeeded in being transmitted exactly as the author had penned it, and each copy that was made invariably carried more mistakes than its predecessor.

If, then, you discover that the earliest available copy of a certain book is a thousand years later than the original, you may expect to find that the text has been corrupted fairly considerably. This, as a matter of fact, is what is commonly discovered with regard to ancient writings. The earliest manuscripts of the Greek and Latin classics are usually at least a thousand years later than the originals, and are full of such copyists' errors – although we can claim confidently, nevertheless, in nearly every case that we possess the text substantially as it was first written. "We believe that we have in all essentials an accurate text of the seven extant plays of Sophocles; yet the earliest substantial manuscript upon which it is based was written more than 1400 years after the poet's death." (Kenyon, *Textual criticism of the New Testament*, p. 4.) The oldest MS of Thucydides is about the same interval of time after the original, while in the case of Euripides the interval is 1600 years, in the case of Plato 1300 and in the case of Demosthenes 1200. The Latin writers are somewhat better off than their Greek counterparts in respect of the time interval between autograph and earliest extant MS, but even there the gap is rarely less than 700 years and sometimes much greater, as in the case of Catullus where it is 1600.

This, then, is the situation with regard to the classical Greek and Latin writings. Many hundreds of years stand between their authorship and their oldest surviving MSS, and these MSS accordingly embody a host of corruptions which have crept into the text during that long process of transmission. In spite of this, in most cases we possess the text in reasonably accurate form.

It would be natural to assume that when we turn to the Bible an exactly similar situation will confront us. There are, however, two significant and remarkable differences. For one thing, the earliest Biblical manuscripts that have been found are hundreds of years nearer the date of their "mother originals" than is the case with any other book of ancient times. This is true both of the Old Testament and the New, but in the case of the New Testament the interval is much shorter. There is even a papyrus fragment of St. John's Gospel to be dated about A.D. 120, a mere twenty years or so later than the original.

Even more remarkable is the quite astonishing accuracy with which the Biblical text has been preserved. By virtue of a prodigious amount of investigation and research, including the comparison of hosts of ancient manuscripts and the comparison of innumerable quotations from early Christian writers, scholars have verified that the text of the Bible has come down to us in immeasurably purer form than the text of any other ancient writing. Their researches have established, in fact, that (while rather more errors have found their way into the text of the Old Testament), the New Testament text underlying, say, the Revised Standard Version is at least 99% identical with what was first written.

2. Another thing which has set the Bible apart from all other books and placed it in a category all of its own has been its possession of a remarkable power to influence men's lives and even to change them. This is something which cannot be disputed because instances abound. Perhaps no better collection of

illustrations of this sort of thing can be cited than is given by A. M. Chirgwin's book *The Bible and World Evangelism*. It includes a number of reports of men whose lives underwent radical change simply through reading the Bible. Let me quote only three.

An American ex-convict was on the way to rejoin his old gang to plan another burglary. En route he picked a man's pocket and sought a quiet place to examine his spoils. To his disgust he discovered that he had stolen a New Testament but, having time to kill, he idly turned over its pages. The book gripped him, and he read on and on. A few hours later he kept his rendezvous with his old companions – but it was to tell them he was finished with crime.

A man called Signor Antonio lived in Brazil. For some time a friend had been urging the claims of Christ upon him and one day this friend gave him a Bible. Signor Antonio took the Bible home but only to burn it. In order that the Bible would burn more easily, he opened it out. He happened to open it at the Sermon on the Mount and some of the words caught his eye and held his attention. He started to read and he read on through the night. As dawn was breaking he stood up and said, "I believe".

In a forest in Sicily a colporteur was waylaid by a brigand who ordered him to light a fire and burn his books. The colporteur asked if he might be permitted to read aloud a short extract from each book before he put it into the flames. The brigand could see no harm in this and gave his permission. From one book the colporteur read the Twenty-third Psalm, from another he read the Parable of the Good Samaritan, from yet another he read part of the Sermon on the Mount, and so on. At the end of each extract the brigand said, "That's a good book; we won't burn that one; give it to me." In the end not one book was burned and the brigand took them all away with him. Years later the brigand encountered the colporteur again – but now he was a Christian minister; and he said, "It was the reading of your books that did it."

3. A further mark of the Bible's claim to uniqueness is the way in which it has all along maintained a position in the forefront of public interest which it has not yet surrendered. It is nearly nineteen hundred years since the Bible was completed, but it is still, as it has been for so long, the world's "best-seller".

It is remarkable that such an old book should still be in demand at all, but that it should be in such worldwide and such clamorous demand is almost too remarkable for belief. The fact is, however, unmistakable, as the annual returns of the Bible Societies, the publishers and the booksellers never fail to assure us. No book in all the world sells so many copies as the Bible.

This fact in itself might seem to be sufficient demonstration that the voice of the Bible is widely listened to today. But it could be argued, and is, that the number of copies of the Bible sold annually gives no real indication of the place and influence it commands in twentieth-century life. Bought it may be but read it is not, not much at any rate, so the critics allege. The voice of the Bible, they say, is reduced in our day to a mere whisper that is audible only to a very few.

No one in his senses would dare to assume that every Bible purchased was actually read. Each year many copies are bought for a variety of reasons other than the intention to read them. Many Bibles in homes throughout the world are rarely handled except to be dusted and a great many more get an airing only when they are taken to church. But when every allowance is made, the fact must still remain that even today, in the latter half of the twentieth century, more people read the Bible, seriously read the Bible, than read any other single book.

My personal conviction that even today a great many people read the Bible and read it carefully and regularly is reinforced by the fact that so many copies are sold of versions other than the Authorised Version. If the "best-selling" characteristic of the Bible is to be explained entirely, or even chiefly, in terms of "show" or custom or anything of that sort, this is a fact for which it is extremely difficult to account.

Modern translations of the Bible like the Revised Standard Version, the New English Bible, the Good News Bible and the rest do not have the prestige value that still belongs to a copy of the Authorised Version. Yet these modern translations are selling in enormous numbers. I for one cannot imagine modern translations of the Bible being bought in large numbers unless it was for the purpose of being read.

It seems to me beyond reasonable doubt that the Bible not only has a buying public in excess of any other book but even today has an actual readership of unequalled size. In other words, very many people in our modern world are listening to its voice.

Whether or not they understand what it says, or believe it, or pay any real heed to it are, however, different questions and we move on now to examine them.

2

WHERE ARE THE FUNDAMENTALISTS?

Some reckon that the Bible is to be understood in terms of an attitude which is often, though loosely, referred to as "fundamentalism". This view of the Bible regards all its contents, without discrimination, as the actual words of God. It is also referred to as the Verbal Inspiration or Literal Inerrancy view.

It may be dangerous to employ this term "fundamentalism" because people use it with different shades of meaning and the whole business of using labels to describe people and their ideas is always fraught with danger. But sometimes it is necessary and at other times, although not strictly necessary, it is convenient and helpful.

For the sake of accuracy and clarity, however, it may be wise to point out that, strictly speaking, the term "fundamentalism" belongs to a movement that took its rise in the USA earlier in the twentieth century. This movement was begun with the avowed aim of defending the original gospel understood literally and of urging the churches to preach this literal interpretation. Twelve pamphlets were published, between 1910 and 1915, defending the literal inerrancy of the Bible, the virgin birth, the deity of Jesus, his physical resurrection, the atoning sacrifice of Calvary, and Jesus' second coming in bodily form. These pamphlets were called "The Fundamentals" and this title gave birth to the name "Fundamentalism".

A precise, historical usage of the term would confine it to this particular movement and its adherents, and would represent all the doctrines defended in "The Fundamentals"; but the name has been largely taken over to designate that verbal inspiration view of the Bible which is one of its characteristics. While the name may be comparatively modern, the attitude to scripture for which it stands is ancient. It existed even in the pre-Christian time, for the Rabbis of later Judaism insisted that the Old Testament scriptures were the actual words of God. The Christian Church began to adopt this Rabbinic attitude at quite an early stage (there are hints of it already in the later books of the New Testament) and in time extended it to include the New Testament as well as the Old.

The idea developed further in the Western than in the Eastern Church, and we find the Church of Rome eventually giving definition to it at the Council of Trent (1545-1567) by declaring that the whole body of scripture, as well as a body of unwritten tradition, had been given "at the dictation of the Holy Spirit". The Vatican Council of 1869-70 repeated the Tridentine phrase "at the dictation of the Holy Spirit"; and in 1893 Leo XIII repeated it again in his encyclical Providentissimus Deus:

> All the books and the whole of each book which the Church receives as sacred and canonical were written at the dictation of the Holy Spirit, and so far is it from being possible that any error can co-exist with divine inspiration that not only does the latter in itself exclude all error, but excludes and rejects it with the same necessity as attaches to the impossibility that God Himself, who is the supreme Truth, should be the author of any error whatever.[1]

The doctrine of the verbal inspiration of scripture was not left behind when the Reformation arrived but continued into the new Churches and came there, indeed, in certain quarters at least, to greater strength and power than it had ever known. This circumstance is something of a paradox since the original Reformers did not themselves subscribe to the theory. Luther, for instance, did not regard the Bible as containing the Word of God in the sense that the words of the Bible were to be equated with the very words of God. In his opinion the written word of scripture was to be judged according to the extent that the gospel was to be found in it, which would be sometimes more, sometimes less.

It was the second generation of Reformers, Calvin in particular, who enunciated that belief in God's having verbally inspired the scriptures which came to take possession of most of the Reformed field; and so it came about that in practice – although not, to begin with at least, in theory – the Reformation meant the substitution of Infallible Book for Infallible Church and Infallible Pope. It is this view of the Bible which is nowadays commonly called "fundamentalist". It declares the Bible to contain the Word of God in the sense that its words are to be equated with God's words. The Bible is God's Book in the sense that "the authors wrote word for word what God intended"[2] and "that every scriptural statement is therefore to be received as a divine utterance".[3] Every paragraph, every sentence, every word of the Bible, from Genesis to Revelation, has been wholly given by God so that all of it is, ipso facto, infallible and inerrant.

It claims to be the key to the proper understanding

of the Bible and would claim, too, that this key
unlocks the door to an understanding which is both
simple and unambiguous. Many think, on the contrary, that the fundamentlist view, so-called, makes
the Bible at times extraordinarily difficult to understand, and that in fact, if that view is to be strictly
adopted, if the words of the Bible are to be equated
always with the very words of God, the Bible's
intelligibility is seriously impaired.

The odd thing is that in practice there does not
appear to be anyone who thoroughly adheres to this
fundamentalist view of the Bible. It seems to be one
to which many give theoretical consent but not full
practical allegiance.

It is commonly held that, broadly speaking,
readers of the Bible may be separated into two
categories. On the one hand, there are those who
accept the Bible as totally the Word of God and, on
the other hand, there are those who reckon that the
Word of God is not to be found uniformly throughout
the whole Bible. On the one hand, those who believe
that all the scriptures have come from God word for
word and, on the other, those who believe that it is
incorrect to say that "the Biblical writers were
completely controlled by the Holy Spirit".[4] On the one
hand, those who regard every part of the Bible as
authoritative for Christian faith and life and, on the
other, those who discriminate with regard to what is
to be considered authoritative.

I suggest, however, that the first of these categories
is largely, if not entirely, imaginary. Many, it is true,
affirm that the Bible is *entirely* the Word of God, and,
as such, "authoritative without qualification".[5] But
do they in fact accept it as such? Is it not the case that

in the event every reader of the Bible – *every* reader, whatever his theology – exercises discrimination towards it?

Some may doubt this statement. I plead with them not to condemn it before they have read further and taken note of the evidence. For this is not a *theory* I seek to prove but a matter of *fact* I hope to make plain. At this juncture I am not concerned with the merits or demerits of the fundamentalist point of view. For the moment I am occupied only with the question of whether or not, in practice, there is any rigid adherence to it. The following illustrations, gathered more or less at random, would appear to make plain that there is not.

We turn first to the Mosaic Law and look at some of the commands recorded in the Book of Leviticus. Leviticus 11: 1-8 reads: "And the Lord said to Moses and Aaron, 'Say to the people of Israel, These are the living things which you may eat among all the beasts that are on the earth. Whatever parts the hoof and is cloven-footed and chews the cud, among the animals, you may eat. Nevertheless among those that chew the cud or part the hoof, you shall not eat these: The camel, because it chews the cud but does not part the hoof, is unclean to you. And the rock badger, because it chews the cud but does not part the hoof, is unclean to you. And the hare, because it chews the cud but does not part the hoof, is unclean to you. And the swine, because it parts the hoof and is cloven-footed but does not chew the cud, is unclean to you. Of their flesh you shall not eat, and their carcasses you shall not touch; they are unclean to you'."

What Christian takes these regulations as binding upon him? Do any of us, for example, seriously

consider it to be God's will that we should refrain
from eating bacon?

In Leviticus 12:2ff. we read: "If a woman con-
ceives, and bears a male child. . .on the eighth day
the flesh of his foreskin shall be circumcised. . .and
when the days of her purifying are completed. . .she
shall bring to the priest. . .a lamb a year old for a
burnt offering, and a young pigeon or a turtledove for
a sin offering." Christian parents, however, do not
regard it as obligatory to have their sons circumcised
nor do Christian mothers think of making the offerings mentioned here after the birth of a child.

Chapter 23 lays down instructions concerning the
feasts that the Lord desires to be kept – Sabbath,
Passover, Pentecost, Atonement, Tabernacles. What
Christian considers himself under obligation to
observe these? It might be pointed out that the
Sabbath is kept by Christians. This, however, merely
confirms my point. I am attempting to demonstrate
that every Christian, in practice, whether fully aware
of it or not, adopts a selective attitude towards what
the Bible says. It is surely doing just that to keep the
Sabbath but ignore the other feasts mentioned side
by side with it. (In most cases anyway the Sabbath
regulations are transferred to Sunday, but we shall
be looking at this later.)

Many similar illustrations could be quoted from
Leviticus but these are enough to show that the
injunctions it contains are not regarded by any
Christian as universally binding. In other words, no
one here attempts strict adherence to the fundamentalist position.

This is not a case of Christians failing to fulfil what
they acknowledge as their duty. It is unlikely that

any of us succeeds, for instance, in obeying perfectly Christ's command to love our enemies; but we recognise, nevertheless, that it is obligatory upon us. The position with regard to the Leviticus laws is quite different. Here it is not a matter of failing in accepted duty, but a matter of refusing to accept these laws as our duty at all. That is to say, all Christians, fundamentalists included, discriminate with regard to these laws and refuse them the authority they give to other parts of the Bible.

Some readers may object that these commands are obviously not intended to have relevance or authority for Christians. They are commands given by God under the old dispensation, instructions given to the people of Israel and meant for them alone, ordinances belonging to the law which has now, of course, been superseded by the gospel. This may be all very well but again merely corroborates the point. To make this objection is to admit the principle of selectiveness and represent the Bible as not being all on the same level of authority.

In any case, the argument brought forward by such objectors would be fully valid only if Christians counted all of the Mosaic Law as being superseded. Christians, however, commonly accept parts of the Law as binding. They regard the Ten Commandments, for instance, as obligatory for the Christian. But the Ten Commandments are part of this same body of Law which the Pentateuch (the first five books of the Old Testament) records as having been transmitted from God through Moses to the people of Israel. This means to say that Christians accept as binding something that stands at one point in the Mosaic Law but do not accept as binding things that

stand alongside it – despite the fact that the Ten
Commandments were addressed to the people of
Israel just as much as were the commandments
about food and about childbirth and about the feasts.
This is surely to discriminate.

I am not, remember, arguing the rights or wrongs
of this discrimination. I am not saying that a man is
wrong to adhere to the Ten Commandments while
dispensing with the practice of abstaining from
bacon. There may be perfectly sound justification for
the Christian so to act; but I am concerned to make
the point that all Christians practise some measure of
discrimination regarding what the Bible has to say.

The Ten Commandments themselves provide us
with another illustration of how universal is this
practice of discrimination. Christians accept the Ten
Commandments as binding, but most Christians do
not accept them all as they stand. The fourth
commandment (Exodus 20: 8-10) says: "Remember
the sabbath day to keep it holy. Six days you shall
labour and do all your work; but the seventh day is a
sabbath to the Lord your God." This commandment
refers to the day that we know as Saturday, the
seventh day of the week. Nearly all Christians, on the
other hand, attempt to observe the requirements of
this commandment with regard to *Sunday*, the first
day of the week. Some principle of discrimination
must be at work when a man can regard himself as
rigidly obeying a law and yet, at the same time,
transfer its requirements from the appointed day to
another. This may well be a perfectly correct thing to
do but the man who does it is showing discrimination.

The reader may feel that my illustrations have
been too much confined to matters of ritual and of

ceremony. He may contend that the things of out-
ward observance which God commanded upon the
Israelites were of local and temporary importance
and that it was only the moral injunctions, such as
the Ten Commandments, that were intended to have
abiding authority. Two things must be said in reply.
First, to distinguish in this way between moral and
ceremonial regulations in the Bible is itself to practise
that kind of discrimination, the universal existence of
which among Christians is all that at the moment I
am concerned to demonstrate. Second, when we turn
our attention to the moral regulations, we find that
no Christian accepts all of these as totally and
inerrantly the word and will of God, but that all
practise discrimination towards them also.

Deuteronomy 15: 1-2, for instance, gives an instruction concerning the wiping out of debts. It says:
"At the end of every seven years you shall grant a
release. And this is the manner of the release: every
creditor shall release what he has lent to his
neighbour; he shall not exact it of his neighbour, his
brother, because the Lord's release has been proclaimed." How many Christians take this seriously
and attempt to translate it into practice?

In Deuteronomy 21: 18-21 we find an injunction
concerning the treatment to be administered to a
wayward son: "If a man has a stubborn and rebellious son, who will not obey the voice of his father
or the voice of his mother, and, though they chastise
him, will not give heed to them, then his father and
mother shall take hold of him and bring him out to
the elders of his city at the gate of the place where he
lives, and they shall say to the elders of his city, 'This
our son is stubborn and rebellious, he will not obey

our voice; he is a glutton and a drunkard.' Then all
the men of the city shall stone him to death with
stones; so you shall purge the evil from your midst;
and all Israel shall hear, and fear." This is plain
enough but no one considers for a moment that this is
the procedure expected of Christian parents and of
the Christian community.

Included in the same list of moral statutes is one
which decrees that the punishment for a couple
discovered in adultery shall be death: "If a man is
found lying with the wife of another man, both of
them shall die, the man who lay with the woman, and
the woman" (Deuteronomy 22: 22). No Christian
today considers that obedience to this practice would
be obedience to the will of God.

Deuteronomy 25: 5 lays it down that if a man should
live in the same house as his married brother and the
brother dies childless, it is that man's duty to marry his
brother's widow. "If brothers dwell together, and one
of them dies and has no son, the wife of the dead shall
not be married outside the family to a stranger; her
husband's brother shall. . .take her as his wife." Does
any reader of the Bible look on this as binding on a
Christian placed in the same circumstance today?

Whatever is to commend the fundamentalist view of
the Bible, the fact appears plain that in practice no one
strictly holds by it. It may be said, perhaps, that it is not
quite fair to arrive at this conclusion by reference to the
Mosaic Law alone, inasmuch as that law was intended
only for the Israelites and has clearly been superseded
by the gospel of Christ. This may be perfectly true but I
have already taken pains to point out that, so far from
casting suspicion on the validity of my conclusion, it
merely serves to confirm it.

To say that the law is superseded by the gospel and that, therefore, the demands of the law are not binding upon Christians is to practise discrimination with regard to the Bible and say that *this* is on a higher level than *that* or, to put it otherwise, to say that X is more truly the Word of God for us today than Y is. What is more, I also pointed out that, in any case, Christians do not simply turn their backs completely on the regulations of the law. The situation is more complex than that. Christians accept some of these regulations as having authority and some as having none and this cannot by any means be interpreted as rigid adherence to the fundamentalist view.

At the same time, this is much too important a matter for us to be satisfied with a conclusion reached on what may appear to some a too narrow basis. Accordingly, we look now at other parts of the Bible to ascertain whether they, too, contain passages concerning which there is universal discrimination. We turn first to what the Old Testament says about the doings and the nature of God. If a man is to be a thorough-going fundamentalist he must take *everything* that the Old Testament says concerning God to be wholly accurate; but nobody, it would appear, fulfils this condition.

Genesis (17: 9-14) records the institution of the circumcision law and represents God as uttering these words: "Every male among you shall be circumcised. . .he that is eight days old among you shall be circumcised;. . .Any uncircumcised male who is not circumcised in the flesh of his foreskin shall be cut off from his people; he has broken my covenant." It is not clear whether the uncircumcised child is to be killed or excommunicated, but, in either event, the punishment to be inflicted on him is one of the utmost severity. Does any Christian reader of the Bible take it as an accurate representation of the nature of God that he should pass such a severe sentence upon a child who patently was not in the least degree responsible for his failure to be circumcised?

A similar illustration is afforded by the incident narrated in Exodus 4: 24-26: "At a lodging place on the way the Lord met him [Moses] and sought to kill him. Then Zipporah took a flint and cut off her son's foreskin, and touched Moses' feet with it, and said, 'Surely you are a bridegroom of blood to me!' So he let him alone." God appears here as one who, for no apparent reason, sets about killing a man on sight and is appeased only by the man's wife hurriedly circumcising her son. Is there anyone who accepts this as an accurate representation of the nature of the God and Father of the Lord Jesus Christ?

The seventh chapter of Joshua tells of the sin of Achan. On account of this sin, God commanded that not only Achan himself but all his family as well should be put to death; and this sentence was duly carried out. No one at all sets this on the same level as the revelation of God's nature in Jesus Christ – but that is what a strict fundamentalist attitude would demand.

Let us look now at some matters of doctrine and first at the doctrine of immortality. On this question the Old Testament has many things to say that no Christian really takes in the fundamentalist sense of infallible and inerrant.[6] In Ecclesiastes 3: 19, for instance, we read: "For the fate of the sons of men and the fate of beasts is the same; as one dies, so dies the other. They all have the same breath, and man has no advantage over the beasts; for all is vanity"; and later in the same book (9: 5) are these words: "For the living know that they will die, but the dead know nothing, and they have no more reward; but the memory of them is lost." There are many other sayings in the Old Testament of a similar character. There is, for instance, Psalm 88: 11-12: "Is thy steadfast love declared in the grave, or thy faithfulness in Abaddon? Are thy wonders known in the darkness, or thy saving help in the land of forgetfulness?" and Psalm 39: 13: "Look away from me, that I may know gladness, before I depart and be no more!" To take these sayings as the infallible and inerrant word of God would be to deny the Christian belief in the life everlasting.

All our illustrations so far have been taken from the Old Testament but before I close the chapter we glance briefly at the New. When we do, it is to discover that even with regard to it nobody appears to adopt a completely fundamentalist position. True, there is nothing like the same amount of discrimination practised towards it as there is towards the Old Testament, but even here all are selective at some point or other. In practice, then, no one accepts even the New Testament as being wholly the words of God, infallible and inerrant.

Here, for instance, is the view of marriage expressed by St. Paul in his first letter to the Corinthians (7: 1ff.): "It is well for a man not to touch a woman. But because of the temptation to immorality, each man should have his own wife and each woman her own husband. . . .To the unmarried and the widows I say that it is well for them to remain single as I do. But if they cannot exercise self-control, they should marry. For it is better to marry than to be aflame with passion." This is not a very lofty view of marriage. Paul looks on marriage as little more than a legalising of the release of physical lust. Does any Christian today accept that view? Would not all Christians – even those who choose to remain celibate – look on marriage quite differently and regard it as "a holy estate, instituted by God. . .ordained for the life-long companionship, help and comfort, which husband and wife ought to have of each other"?[7]

From all that we have examined in this chapter the fact emerges plainly and unmistakably that no one accepts, in reality, every word of the Bible as "the utterance of God 'who cannot lie', whose word once spoken abides for ever."[8] Many are strong in their advocacy of the fundamentalist understanding of the Bible and may be equally strong in their belief that they strictly adhere to it.

Is there, however, anybody who actually takes and acts upon the Bible as totally and perfectly, from beginning to end, the words of God?

NOTES AND REFERENCES

1   John Baillie, *The Idea of Revelation in Recent Thought*, p. 31.
2   J. I. Packer, *Fundamentalism and the Word of God*, p. 79.
3   Ibid. p. 85.
4   Ibid. p. 78.
5   Ibid. p. 72.
6   Ibid. p. 96. "Scripture is termed infallible and inerrant to express the conviction that all its teaching is the utterance of God 'who cannot lie', whose word, once spoken, abides for ever, and that therefore it may be trusted implicitly."
7   *The Book of Common Order* of The Church of Scotland (1940), p. 154.
8   Packer, op. cit. p.95.

3

IS DISCRIMINATION JUSTIFIED?

We have observed that in practice all Christians exercise a discriminative attitude towards the scriptures. We must now ask whether that discrimination is justified; if it is, the fundamentalist view of the Bible will be seen to obscure rather than to clarify the message of the Bible today.

Do the Scriptures Claim Verbal Inspiration for Themselves?
The scriptures do not claim for themselves that "the authors wrote word for word what God intended".[1] There are, indeed, some references in the New Testament to divine authority of scripture but we must remember that the New Testament authors were referring not to their own writings but to the scriptures of the Old Testament. By the time of Jesus, the Old Testament writings were generally regarded as the authoritative voice of God – a fact, incidentally, which makes the attitude of Jesus all the more significant, as we shall see – but neither the Old Testament nor the New Testament books claim for themselves that they are the very words of God.

Even if they did, that would not settle the question of their verbal inspiration. One is scarcely entitled to agree that "the Biblical writers were *completely* controlled by the Holy Spirit" simply because they said they were. This would be to prove one's point by assuming it. But the fact is that nowhere in scripture is the claim to plenary inspiration made. On the contrary the writers repeatedly represent themselves as having real personal responsibility for what they write. When, for instance, Luke claims reliability for his Gospel on the grounds that he has made a careful investigation and a thorough sifting of previous writings and earlier sources to aid its compilation (Luke 1: 1-4), how can we reconcile this claim with a belief on his part that he was being verbally inspired and that the Holy Spirit would preserve him from all error?

Jesus' Attitude to Scripture

The Bible of Jesus' day was what we know as the Old Testament (the New Testament, of course, had not yet been written). If Jesus' attitude to it was what I have designated fundamentalist, we must at once ask why all do not maintain that position. If, on the other hand, Jesus' attitude was not fundamentalist, the conclusion becomes inevitable that all should abandon that position.

What then, is the situation? Our Lord's use of the Old Testament scriptures makes it clear that he valued them very highly and found the pattern of his mission outlined in them; but it is just as clear that he did not regard them as literally inerrant. Indeed, little could be plainer than the fact that he exercised discrimination towards them.

Here, for instance, in the words of Jesus is what amounts to an emphatic renunciation of the Old Testament laws dealing with clean and unclean food. "There is nothing outside a man which by going into him can defile him; but the things which come out of a man are what defile him. . . .Do you not see that whatever goes into a man from outside cannot defile him, since it enters, not his heart but his stomach, and so passes on?" (Mark 7: 15, 18, 19). The Mosaic Law states explicitly and emphatically in God's name that certain foods are unclean and that the person who eats them is defiled. In this passage, however, Jesus pointedly and deliberately sweeps these regulations aside as being not only unimportant but even misleading. There can be no doubt that in Jesus' eyes these Old Testament regulations, although they had been attributed to God, were not the Word of God at all. They had been understood as such and had been recorded in good faith as such but they did not, in Jesus' opinion, represent the will of God and so he discarded them.

Another illustration is given by Jesus' attitude to the Mosaic Law of divorcement. Deuteronomy 24: 1 says: "When a man takes a wife and marries her, if then she finds no favour in his eyes because he has found some indecency in her, he writes her a bill of divorce and puts it in her hand and sends her out of his house, and she departs out of his house." This was not to Jesus the will of God inerrantly set down in writing. To him it was an imperfect precept that must now be replaced by a better, and so he said to his disciples, "What therefore God has joined together, let not man put asunder. . . .Whoever divorces his wife and marries another, commits adultery against her, and if she divorces her husband and marries another, she commits adultery" (Mark 10: 9, 11, 12).

The plainest and best illustration of the fact that Jesus was no fundamentalist is to be found in his Sermon on the Mount – and having quoted this we

C

need quote no other. Revealing as it does the new ethical order that Jesus wishes to introduce, the whole of this wonderful teaching is a sentence of judgment upon the old law enshrined in the Old Testament. Early in the Sermon Jesus declares, "Think not that I have come to abolish the law and the prophets; I have come not to abolish them but to fulfil them" (Matthew 5: 17): but, at the same time, he left no doubt that the fulfilment of the law which he desired was not an adherence to its existing regulations but a carrying to completion of its abiding elements. This meant a passing beyond and an abandonment of a number of features of the law that were now become irrelevant or unnecessary or even a hindrance to the fulfilment that Jesus purposed.

As a result we find, for instance, that five times in the fifth chapter of St. Matthew Jesus uses the same striking antithesis to make some kind of correction to the Old Testament law. At verse 27, at verse 31, at verse 33, at verse 38 and at verse 43, Jesus makes a quotation from the Old Testament, prefacing it each time with the introductory words, "You have heard. . ."; and, on each occasion, follows it up with a comment of his own, introduced by the phrase, "But I say to you. . .". These are clearly not the words and that was clearly not the attitude of one who held to the view of scripture that fundamentalism stands for.

In face of this it is extremely difficult to try to maintain that Jesus regarded "the whole of the Old Testament. . .as binding on his hearers"[2] or that he looked on it "as the authoritative written utterance of God, abidingly true and trustworthy".[3]

This is not to deny that Jesus valued the Old Testament highly. Beyond doubt it was for him, as it was for his contemporaries, the Book of God. He was steeped in its contents and in its pages he was able to discover the pattern of his own mission of redemptive suffering. Nevertheless, it is beyond doubt also that the Old Testament was not for Jesus the Book of God in the sense that God supervised its writing in such a way that it contained no error, no inadequacy, no imperfection and that its every word was equally the Word of God. Jesus' use of the Old Testament scriptures leaves no doubt that in many respects what they had to say was inadequate and imperfect, and sometimes far off the mark. Part of the purpose of his mission was to put these things right and to reveal plainly and fully the truths about God, his nature and his will, which the Old Testament records enshrined only in partial, distorted, or embryonic form. The attitude of Jesus to the Old Testament was unmistakably an attitude of careful discrimination.

Discrepancies

Turning to the Bible as a whole we discover that it contains many things which make nonsense of the fundamentalist position. From the standpoint of verbal inspiration it is, for instance, quite impossible to account adequately for the circumstance that, on numerous occasions, one part of the Biblical record is found to differ in details from another when dealing with the same fact. Such features of the Biblical writings, there for all to see, are incompatible with the idea that every word of scripture came directly and without error from God.

Little purpose is to be served by quoting numerous instances of this sort of thing and I merely indicate what I have in mind. There is, for example, Genesis 6: 19, where God commands Noah, "And of every living thing of all flesh, you shall bring two of every sort into the ark"; whereas in Genesis 7: 2, the command reads, "Take with you seven pairs of all clean animals. . .and a pair of the animals that are not clean." Again, 2 Kings 24: 8 says that Jehoiachin was eighteen years old when he became king; whereas 2 Chronicles 36: 9 says that he was eight.

There are many such discrepancies of detail in the Bible, especially in the Old Testament, and their presence makes it impossible to think of the Bible as the actual words of God. It may be said in reply that none of the discrepancies is of any great importance — and that is perfectly true. In themselves they are of little consequence. Nevertheless, they flatly contradict the fundamentalist view of scripture. Such discrepancies, however minor and however unimportant, are sufficient to make it manifestly absurd "that the authors wrote word for word what God intended"[4] – unless we are prepared to think of God contradicting himself.

Of similar significance is the fact that we find the New Testament writers frequently misquoting the Old Testament. Out of a total of 275 quotations there are only 53 in which the Hebrew Bible, the Septuagint (the Greek translation of the Old Testament), and the New Testament agree word for word. In no less than 99 of these quotations the New Testament differs both from the Hebrew and from the Septuagint. This also is quite incompatible with the view that "the Biblical writers were completely controlled by the Holy Spirit". It is inconceivable that the Holy Spirit should be responsible for misquotations.

Advocates of the fundamentalist position sometimes say, "the majority of these small discrepancies and residual problems are clearly due to defects in transmission and to similar explicable causes."[5] This is much too facile an explanation of the facts but, even if it were conceded, it would make little or no difference to the significance of the matter so far as verbal inspiration is concerned. Not only "the majority" but every single one of such discrepancies would require to be so explained. If even one of them remains as part of the original text, the fundamentalist position is rendered untenable.

In any event, even if every discrepancy could be so explained, the situation would become little more congenial for the fundamentalist. For him to maintain, on the one hand, that it was the original text which was verbally inspired and totally inerrant and, on the other hand, to maintain that we do not possess the original text in entirely accurate form, is to relinquish what he is striving to secure. To argue in these terms is to admit that the Bible as we have it cannot be accepted as word for word God-given. (To argue in these terms, incidentally, does little honour to God. For if God had seen fit to create a totally inerrant text of his words, would he not also have ensured that it was perfectly preserved from corruption?)

We do not, however, require to depend on the above argument, valid though it is, to demonstrate that the internal evidence of the Bible is enough to rule plenary inspiration out of court. So far we have considered no more than a few examples of discrepancies

of detail between different parts of the Bible in their
account of the same facts. When we look more closely
we find that there are much more telling discrepancies
than these. We find, for instance, different advice
being given and different judgments being made
concerning the same thing or the same person – a
feature of the records which can scarcely be reconciled
with the idea that "the authors wrote word for word
what God intended".

We find, for example, that Psalm 104: 15 speaks
approvingly of wine as something "to gladden the
heart of man"; while Proverbs 20: 1 speaks of it in
disapproving terms. "Wine is a mocker, strong drink
a brawler; and whoever is led astray by it is not
wise." A similar illustration to this is given by the fact
that St. Paul commands, "And do not get drunk with
wine" (Ephesians 5: 18), while Proverbs commands,
"Give strong drink to him who is perishing, and wine
to those in bitter distress; let them drink and forget
their poverty, and remember their misery no more"
(31: 6-7).

More significant still is the fact that there are
disagreements on such fundamental matters as the
nature and will of God. If the Bible were really the
actual words of God, then surely it must speak from
first to last with a unanimous voice on matters like
these. Demonstrably it does not. In Deuteronomy
20: 16, 17, we read: "But in the cities of these people
that the Lord your God gives you for an inheritance,
you shall save alive nothing that breathes, but you
shall utterly destroy them, the Hittites and the
Amorites, the Canaanites and the Perizzites, the
Hivites and the Jebusites, as the Lord your God has
commanded." These words present one picture of

God. It is quite a different picture that is given when St. John says, "God is love" (1 John 4: 8); or when Jesus says, "Love your enemies and pray for those who persecute you" (Matthew 5: 44).

Many instances of a similar kind could be cited and many points of a similar character could be made. Time and again the representation of God that is found on a certain page of the Old Testament is more or less plainly contradicted by what is said of him in the New Testament or even in another part of the Old Testament. Some of the earlier writings of the Old Testament, for example, look on him as only one god among many, even though pre-eminent over the others; later writings of the Old Testament share with the New Testament the realisation that he is God alone. Some of the earlier writings of the Old Testament encourage the notion that he is interested only in the Jews; later writings are moving towards that knowledge of his world-wide love which the New Testament declares in all the glory of its fulness. Some of the earlier writings of the Old Testament leave little room for the idea that he might be interested in men individually; the later writers have begun to grasp the truth, shown forth in the gospel of Christ, that he loves every single one "as if he had only one to love".

Not only with regard to points of fact, not only with regard to the conception of the nature and the will of God, but on other matters, too, we find discrepancies between one part of scripture and another. This is found, for example, to a quite marked extent in relation to the doctrine of immortality, as we have already noted (see p. 22).

Such passages as earlier quoted – and many others

of like nature can be culled from the pages of the Old
Testament – teach with unmistakable plainness that
there is no personal immortality and that the grave is
final. How different from the sentiment expressed in
them is the sentiment of Job 19: 25: "For I know that
my Redeemer lives, and at last he will stand upon the
earth; and after my skin has been thus destroyed,
then from my flesh I shall see God." How different
again such New Testament words as, for instance, in
John 14: 2, 19: "In my Father's house are many
rooms; if it were not so, would I have told you that I
go to prepare a place for you?. . .because I live, you
will live also"; or in 1 Thessalonians 4: 13-14: "But
we would not have you ignorant, brethren, concerning those who are asleep, that you may not grieve as
others do who have no hope. For since we believe
that Jesus died and rose again, even so, through
Jesus, God will bring with him those who have fallen
asleep."

The statements quoted above are so irreconcilable
in their view of life after death that it is difficult to see
how any theory of verbal inspiration can survive in
face of their conflict. By no stretch of imagination are
they able to be all and each construed as the exact
and inerrant words of God.

There would seem, therefore, to be no necessity to
bring forward any more of the many similar illustrations that are lying to hand. It may be worthwhile,
however, to add one further point. So far our
examples have been restricted to passages from the
Old Testament at variance with other passages of
scripture, either in the Old Testament or in the New
Testament. It may appear from this that, while the
theory of verbal inspiration must be dispensed with

so far as the Old Testament is concerned, it may yet be possible to maintain it with regard to the New. That is not so. Although the New Testament approximates more closely than the Old to that state of inerrancy which the fundamentalist theory demands, it does not fully attain it.

The New Testament also has points of fact on which different passages give different details. For instance, the genealogy of Jesus as given by St. Matthew does not agree exactly with that given by St. Luke; and the first three gospels place the "cleansing of the temple" at the end of the ministry of Jesus (Mark 11: 15-17; Matthew 21: 12-14; Luke 19: 45-46) whereas the fourth gospel puts it at the beginning (John 2: 13-17). Admittedly, this sort of thing is far less frequent in the New Testament than in the Old; admittedly, the instances quoted and others like them are of no major importance and do not detract from the basic trustworthiness of the gospel narratives (indeed, they rather serve to confirm it); nevertheless, they are undeniably inconsistent with literal inerrancy.

We take note of one more illustration from the New Testament. Even within its pages there are instances where one passage appears to differ from or to put right another on a matter, not of fact, but of opinion or outlook. We find illustration of just this thing in Paul's view of marriage. The Apostle's view of marriage stated in First Corinthians shows considerable difference from that stated in Ephesians.[6]

(It may be noteworthy, since 1 Corinthians has been mentioned, to point out how St. Paul, in the first chapter of that epistle, corrects himself on a point of fact. In verse 14 he says, "I am thankful that I

baptized none of you except Crispus and Gaius"; but
two verses further on he pulls himself up to say, "I
did baptize also the household of Stephanas" – a fact
which he had apparently overlooked when he made
his earlier statement. This is the kind of thing which
frequently happens when a man is writing a letter
but is extremely difficult to understand if God
through his Holy Spirit is supervising word by word
the writing of it.)

It is not a very exalted conception of marriage that
St. Paul expresses in 1 Corinthians 7 (see p. 23).
Marriage is here represented as no more than a poor
second-best to be turned to only if one's physical
desires cannot be restrained. But in Ephesians 5:
22-33 St. Paul gives a quite different and much loftier
view of marriage. There he likens the marriage
relationship to the relationship between Christ and
his Church, in words such as these (v. 25): "Hus-
bands, love your wives, as Christ loved the church
and gave himself up for her."

It is sometimes argued that St. Paul explicitly
states that what he says on marriage in 1 Corinthians
7 is his own opinion and not the voice of God. This
argument is based on the words of verse 6: "I say this
by way of concession, not of command", but it
appears to depend upon a faulty exegesis. The
correct understanding of the verse would seem to be,
not that God has permitted, rather than commanded, Paul to say what he says about marriage;
but that Paul is permitting, not commanding, the
Corinthians to practise the abstinence to which he
refers in the previous verse and of which, apparently,
their letter to him had spoken. It means that Paul is
granting his readers a concession as contrasted with

laying an injunction upon them. They may, if they wish, keep these seasons of abstinence but they are not being ordered to keep them.

In any event, supposing the fudamentalist to be allowed his own interpretation of the verse, it still involves his theory in the gravest difficulty. For it asks us to assume that God would permit one of his agents to introduce his own opinions into a letter that otherwise was a message from himself, and opinions, at that, which were contrary to his mind, as Ephesians must then be taken to imply.

It has, I think, been amply demonstrated that the so-called fundamentalist view of the Bible is not, as claimed, the key to its proper understanding. Such a view often tends to obscure its true meaning and message at many points. The approach that will enable the Bible to speak more clearly to our day has, therefore, to be sought elsewhere.

NOTES AND REFERENCES

1 Packer, *Fundamentalism and the Word of God*, p. 79.
2 D. Johnson, *The Christian and his Bible*. pp. 64-5.
3 Packer, op. cit. p. 59.
4 Ibid. p. 79.
5 Johnson, op. cit. p. 124.
6 Most scholars reckon that Paul was not the author of Ephesians but the point we make here and elsewhere is unaffected by the question of authorship.

4

THE "DEVELOPING REVELATION"

A feature of the Bible writings to which our discussion may have called attention is what is often referred to as the "developing revelation of God", but is much more properly described as the "developing grasp of the revelation of God". This may appear to be a quibble but there is a world of difference. The former suggests that God's self-disclosure was handed out to man piecemeal and perhaps in rather grudging fashion with God allowing himself to be known only a little at a time. The latter makes it much plainer that God was always willing to be fully known but that man was able only bit by bit to apprehend his self-revelation.

The Bible plainly does record such a progressive or devloping understanding of God, his ways and wishes. Jesus' own use of scripture is itself sufficient to make this clear. Recognition of this fact is essential to the proper understanding of the Bible. So important a clue does it provide that we are going to use the whole of the present chapter to look at some examples of this development.

Sovereignty of God

To begin with, there is the Bible's development in the idea of the sovereignty of God. At first the people of Israel saw YAHWEH[1] as no more than *their* God who had proved his worth by leading them to victory in many battles.

Jephthah, for instance, in Judges 11 believes that Chemosh, the god of the people of Ammon, is a real god, who gives his people territory to possess in the same way as YAHWEH gives territory to the people of Israel: "So then the Lord, the God of Israel, dispossessed the Amorites from before his people Israel; and are you to take possession of them? Will you not possess what Chemosh your god gives you to possess? And all that the Lord our God has dispossessed before us, we will possess" (11: 23-24). Jephthah believes that the Lord is a more powerful god than Chemosh but he is a long way short of believing that the Lord is the only god there is.

Again, in 1 Samuel 26: 19, we find that David's appeal to Saul against his banishment contains the lament that to be driven out of YAHWEH's land is to be exiled from his worship: "Now therefore let my lord the king hear the words of his servant. If it is the Lord who has stirred you up against me, may he accept an offering; but if it is men, may they be cursed before the Lord, for they have driven me out this day that I should have no share in the heritage of the Lord, saying, 'Go, serve other gods'." If David is forced to dwell outside the territory of YAHWEH, he will at the same time be forced to enter the service of other gods. To David's mind – as to the minds of those who heard him speak – YAHWEH's sovereignty was restricted to the territory of the Israelites.

The same outlook is found in 2 Kings 5: 17, where Naaman, wishing to worship YAHWEH in his own land, begs for "two mules' burden of earth" to take home to Syria, since YAHWEH's sovereignty is confined to his own soil.

In the earlier stage of religious development which such instances represent, YAHWEH was regarded as a deity of limited scope. He was the god of Israel but not of other nations. These other nations had their own gods who were also real beings and who exercised dominion within their own territories. They were inferior in power to YAHWEH, as was evidenced time after time on the field of battle; but inside their own domain they held full sway and there YAHWEH had no authority. Should a man cross the border of Israel into another nation's territory, and take up residence there, he could no longer continue to worship YAHWEH. YAHWEH had neither part nor place in the land where he now dwelled and so he must worship the god under whose jurisdiction and authority it lay.

This early stage in the understanding of YAHWEH's sovereignty is to be detected in many places in the Old Testament. Gradually, however, that understanding began to grow wider and truer, until at length it was recognised that the sovereignty of YAHWEH extended not only over one nation, nor even a group of nations, but over the whole world. This recognition is given expression, for example, in the book of Amos. The first two chapters depict YAHWEH as having authority and power over each and every nation; and, towards the close of the book, the idea of YAHWEH's world-wide dominion is expressed in a single verse: "Are you not like the Ethiopians to me, O people of Israel? says the Lord. Did I not bring up Israel from the land of Egypt, and the Philistines from Caphtor and the Syrians from Kir?" (9: 7).

This carries us far forward from the old idea of YAHWEH's geographically limited sovereignty. But the pages of the Old Testament carry us further forward still, until we arrive at the recognition that YAHWEH is not merely chief among gods but is, in fact, the only god. Thus we read in Isaiah 44: 8: "Is there a God besides me? There is no Rock; I know not any." With this explicit declaration the religious perception of the Old Testament had come at length to that monotheism which the New Testament everywhere assumes.

The New Testament never needs to argue in favour of monotheism nor does it ever display the slightest doubt about its truth. The later prophets had performed their task too well for that. That YAHWEH is God alone is a truth fundamental to the whole New Testament from beginning to end. All that Jesus did and taught and all that his followers did and taught assumed this. Paul speaks, as it were, for the whole of the New Testament when he says in 1 Corinthians 8: 4, "We know that an idol has no real existence, and that there is no God but one."

Ominipresence of God

There was a similar development of the idea of God's omnipresence. In earlier times YAHWEH was regarded as localised, not only in the sense of being god only of the Israelites and as confined to the territory over which they ruled; but also as being localised within Israel itself and present only in certain places.

At one time his abode was Sinai so that when Moses wished to enter into communion with him he "went up to God, and the Lord called to him out of

the mountain" (Exodus 19: 3). Later his presence
was regarded as being localised to the ark, so that
when, for instance, the tide of battle was running
against them, the Israelites sent for the ark to be
brought to the battlefield, believing that with it came
the presence of YAHWEH, too. 1 Samuel 4: 2-3, for
example, tells us: "The Philistines drew up in line
against Israel, and when the battle spread, Israel was
defeated by the Philistines, who slew about four
thousand men on the field of battle. And when the
troops came to the camp, the elders of Israel said,
'Why has the Lord put us to rout today before the
Philistines? Let us bring the ark of the covenant of the
Lord here from Shiloh, that he may come among us
and save us from the power of our enemies'." The
chapter goes on to tell of the battle being won, after
all, by the Philistines and of the victors carrying off
the ark as part of the spoils of war; and, when the ark
was taken from them, the Israelites believed that the
presence of YAHWEH was taken too.

Later still, YAHWEH's presence was regarded as
belonging to those places that had been consecrated
as shrines to him. If a man wished to enter into
communion with him he had to go up to one of these
shrines and make his offering. In Exodus 20: 24, for
instance, YAHWEH is reported as saying, "An altar
of earth you shall make for me and sacrifice on it your
burnt offerings and your peace offerings, your sheep
and your oxen; in every place where I cause my name
to be remembered I will come to you and bless you."

Gradually men came to see that, just as God's
sovereignty was not contained by physical or
geographical barriers, neither was his presence; and
so we find, for instance, the Psalmist saying,

"Whither shall I go from thy Spirit? Or whither shall I flee from thy presence? If I ascend to heaven, thou art there! If I make my bed in Sheol, thou art there! If I take the wings of the morning and dwell in the uttermost parts of the sea, even there thy hand shall lead me, and thy right hand shall hold me" (Psalm 139: 7-10). In such passages as this the Old Testament reached forward to the truth revealed by Jesus in all its fulness that God is everywhere and available always for every soul who wishes to enter into communion with him.

God's Universal Love

Collateral with the two developments described above, the Old Testament also reveals a development towards the recognition that God cares for every individual of every race. To begin with, the Israelites thought of YAHWEH as exclusively their God and as having, if no enmity, certainly no love for any other race. Starting from this point, we can detect in the Old Testament a two-fold development, a development, on the one hand, of the realisation that God was interested not only in the Jews but in all nations, and a development, on the other hand, of the realisation that God was interested in men not only as nations but as individuals.

YAHWEH was the God of the Israelites – that was the early belief – but he was God of the Israelite nation and had little or no interest in the individuals who comprised it except as they contributed to his purposes for the nation. This is typified by the way in which it is believed that God conferred favour or exacted punishment upon the group to which the individual belonged and not solely upon the

individual himself. So we find that, when Achan
disobeyed the Lord's command by appropriating for
himself some of the booty of Jericho, "The anger of the
Lord burned against the children of Israel" (Joshua 7:
1); and that anger was appeased only when, on Achan
being discovered as the culprit, his whole family was
put to death. "Joshua, and all Israel. . .took Achan
. . .and his sons and daughters. . . .And all Israel
. . .burned them with fire and stoned them with
stones. . .then the Lord turned from his burning
anger" (Joshua 7: 24-26).

This was the primitive stage of the belief – God was
not interested in any nation save Israel and God was
not interested even in the Israelites as individuals.
But as the awareness grew that God had sovereignty
not only over Israel but over every other nation as
well, so the awareness came that he had affection not
only for Israel but for all other nations, too. Thus we
find Isaiah hearing God say, "Blessed be Egypt my
people, and Assyria the work of my hands, and Israel
my heritage."

This dawning awareness pointed forward to the
apprehension of the fuller truth that God had affection not only for all nations but for every individual
within every nation. This, however, was still a long
way off and in Old Testament times it was rarely
glimpsed even as a distant prospect. Even at the
beginning of New Testament times it was still largely
unrecognised. It needed Jesus to make it known.
Nevertheless, we can detect the Old Testament
taking some further steps towards it.

In his eighteenth chapter Ezekiel stoutly main-
tains that it is all wrong to think of God dealing with
men only as groups, pleased or displeased, blessing

or punishing, according as their group action is good or bad. As Ezekiel understood it, YAHWEH was concerned with how the individual behaved. "Behold, all souls are mine; the soul of the father, as well as the soul of the son is mine: the soul that sins shall die. If a man is righteous and does what is lawful and right. . .he shall surely live, says the Lord God" (Ezekiel 18: 4, 5, 9).

It was only a short step from this before Jeremiah caught the vision of God as a being who cared for the individual and with whom the individual could enter into a personal relationship; and so was able to say, "O Lord, my strength and my stronghold, my refuge in the day of trouble" (Jeremiah 16: 19).

This two-strand development towards an awareness of God's real concern for each individual of every nation reached its climax in Jesus. He made it plain that the Father's love embraced every man whatever his race. In Matthew 8: 11, for example, Jesus says, "I tell you, many will come from east and west and sit at table with Abraham, Isaac, and Jacob in the kingdom of heaven"; and few will need to be reminded of John 3: 16: "For God so loved the world that he gave his only Son, that whoever believes in him should not perish but have eternal life."

But perhaps the most vivid portrayal of God's care and concern for every individual is given by Jesus when he says, "Are not five sparrows sold for two pennies? And not one of them is forgotten before God. Why, even the hairs of your head are all numbered. Fear not; you are of more value than many sparrows" (Luke 12: 6-7). The price of sparrows was two for a penny (Matthew 10: 29) and five for two pennies. This is to say, when two pennies' worth was purchased, an extra sparrow was thrown in for nothing. In the eyes of men a sparrow was dirt cheap and yet "not one of them is forgotten before God". The individual man, says Jesus, as he drives his lesson home, is much more precious in God's sight than many sparrows.

Life after Death

One of the best examples the Bible affords of the process of development is given by that growth and enrichment of belief in the future life which we have already noted. In earliest times the Israelites had no real belief in a life beyond the grave; to all intents and purposes life came to an end at that point. A man did not altogether cease to exist but he could no longer be said to *live*; for when he died, he went to Sheol, the abode of all the dead, both good and bad, and Sheol was no more than a place of shadowy existence and of forgetfulness, in which was stripped away all that made life meaningful and glad.

Practically speaking, while death did not mean the complete end of existence, it did mean the end of life; and page after page of the Old Testament stresses the finality of death. "For in death there is no remembrance of thee; in Sheol who can give thee praise?" (Psalm 6: 5); "Look away from me, that I may know gladness, before I depart and be no more!" (Psalm 39: 13); "For Sheol cannot thank thee, death cannot praise thee; those who go down to the pit cannot hope for thy faithfulness" (Isaiah 38: 18).

In those days there was no vision of any real personal immortality among the people of Israel. The only immortality that they knew – and they valued it highly – was that which was theirs in and through their descendants. Thus we find, for instance, a widow woman of Tekoah appealing to David to spare the life of her surviving son, who has murdered his brother; and the basis of her appeal is that, if he is slain, "Thus they would quench my coal which is left, and leave to my husband neither name nor remnant upon the face of the earth" (2 Samuel 14: 7).

Some Psalms, however, show definite glimmerings of belief in a real life after death – such as, for instance, Psalm 49: 15, which says: "But God will ransom my soul from the power of Sheol, for he will receive me" and Psalm 73: 24: "Thou dost guide me with thy counsel, and afterward thou wilt receive me to glory". And this development in the idea of life after death is carried still further forward when Daniel says, "And many of those who sleep in the dust of the earth shall awake, some to everlasting life, and some to shame and everlasting contempt" (12: 2).

Unmistakably, then, we find that there is a clear development in the doctrine of immortality even within the limits of the Old Testament itself. To begin with – and, admittedly, for the most part – the writings of the Old Testament betray no thought of any existence beyond the grave other than the shadowy, "lifeless" post-mortem of Sheol.

Some men, however, came in time to feel that this was not a true picture and were able to catch glimpses, some clearer than others, of what the true picture was. But, even at the best, they do little more than point forward with a somewhat wavering finger to what in the New Testament is set forth in all its richness and in all its certainty, the Christian belief in the "life everlasting".

We see the climax of the development begun in the Old Testament and, at the same time, see how far that climax outreaches the beginning, when we read passages like John 14: 1ff.: "Let not your hearts be troubled; believe in God, believe also in me. In my Father's house are many rooms"; or John 11: 25: "I am the resurrection and the life; he who believes in me, though he die, yet shall he live"; or Romans 8: 35, 37-39: "Who shall separate us from the love of Christ? Shall tribulation, or distress, or persecution, or famine, or nakedness, or peril, or sword?. . .No, in all these things we are more than conquerors through him who loved us. For I am sure that neither death, nor life, nor angels, nor principalities, nor things present, nor things to come, nor powers, nor height, nor depth, nor anything else in all creation, will be able to separate us from the love of God in Christ Jesus our Lord"; or 1 Corinthians 15: 54-55: "When the perishable puts on the imperishable, and the mortal puts on immortality, then shall come to pass the saying that is written: Death is swallowed up in victory. O death, where is thy victory? O death, where is thy sting?"

I have indicated a few illustrations of the development of an idea or a belief in the Bible. There are many others. Their presence confirms the untenability of any theory of verbal inspiration, for that theory would require the Bible to be unanimous throughout in its teaching. God could not possibly be found to speak with different or contradictory voices on the same subject.

It may be thought that these "developments" are always and only a matter of development in, from, and through the Old Testament up to the New

Testament; and that, therefore, the New Testament at least may be taken as being all on the one level of wisdom and truth and authority.

But, while most developments are through the Old Testament to the New, the New Testament displays development on some matters also. To one of these we have, in fact, already referred. In writing to the Corinthians in about A.D. 55, Paul speaks of marriage as no more than, at best, an unfortunate necessity and to be avoided if possible (1 Corinthians 7). But less than ten years later, writing to the Ephesians, he could speak of marriage as a rich and sacred thing (Ephesians 4). This is a minor matter but it is indisputable; and is a further demonstration that, if the Bible is to be properly understood, all thoughts of its being verbally inspired must be laid aside.

NOTES AND REFERENCES

1   YAHWEH was the personal proper name which the Hebrews gave to the deity. It is usually translated in our English Old Testament as "the Lord".

5

THE KEY TO UNDERSTANDING

We have seen that the verbal inspiration attitude to the Bible will not do. We have seen that every Christian, whatever his theory, in practice discriminates in his use and interpretation of the Bible; we have seen that the practice of discrimination is justified, not to say essential, in a right use of the Bible; we have seen that Jesus' own attitude to the scriptures was one of discrimination; and so we have arrived at the stage where we know that the Bible, to be fully intelligible, must be read with a discriminating mind. But we have still to define our principle of discrimination. We have, as it were, discovered the door to the treasure-house of the Bible; we have now to lay hold of the key.

Until and unless we do, all our discussion so far will have been less than useless. Haphazard discrimination, an arbitrary choosing of this and a rejecting of that, would be disastrous. It would result in little more than a breaking down of the Bible into pieces and a selection only of such pieces as appealed to our own likes. This would be to be *in*discriminate in our attitude and the consequence would be that the Bible's chief value would be lost. It would be akin to breaking down a watch into its component parts and leaving it like that; the main and disastrous result would be to render the watch incapable of telling the time.

It may appear that we have, in fact, done no more than break down our "watch" into pieces and that our search for the key to the understanding of the scriptures has not been greatly aided, if at all, by our discussions so far. It may seem that we have done no more than establish what that key is not. Nevertheless, the positive gains of our study are not negligible.

In Chapter Two we discovered that in practice every Christian exercises discrimination towards the Bible and looks on certain parts as without relevance or without validity for his thought and conduct. At the time we did not stop to ask why Christians should reckon this irrelevant or that invalid; but when we do, we find the answer lies in their knowledge of Jesus Christ and of the revelation of God given in him.

We discovered that Christians disregard the Mosaic Law at many points. They pay little heed, for instance, to those regulations that have to do with abstention from "unclean meats" and the reason that they count it no sin to have, say, bacon for breakfast is that Jesus has shown these eating rules to be of no importance for Christian conduct. They make discrimination at this point because of him who said that what defiled a man was not any supposedly unclean thing which he might eat but the evil thoughts and desires that issued from his mind and heart. That is to say, their principle of discrimination is Jesus Christ.

The Mosaic Law contains also a vast and detailed amount of instruction concerning the sacrifices that God's people are to offer in various circumstances. No Christian ever thinks of attempting to obey these instructions and the reason is that Jesus has made plain that the sacrifice which God really wants is the offering of a man's whole being on the altar of his love and service. Here, again, the principle of discrimination is Jesus Christ.

Christians, in the main, do not accept the fourth commandment on its own terms. It is an injunction to keep holy the Sabbath day (i.e. Saturday, the last day of the week), but most Christians keep holy Sunday (the first day of the week). The reason is that Jesus began his Church with his resurrection from the dead on a Sunday and so made Sunday a holier day for the Christian than the Sabbath. Once more the principle of discrimination is Jesus Christ.

We could examine example after example of Christians discriminating with regard to the Mosaic Law and in every case we would find the reason for the discrimination to be their knowledge of Jesus Christ and of the revelation of God given in him.

When we turned from the law we discovered that a number of Old Testament passages depicted God in a way which no Christian would accept as fully true. When, for example, 1 Samuel 15: 2-3 speaks of God commanding the wholesale extermination of the Amalekites, even to the children and the babes in arms, the Christian refuses to accept this record as being true to the real nature of God; and the reason for his refusal is that such conduct cannot be harmonised with the kind of person Jesus has revealed God to be. So it is with passages such as Genesis 7: 9-14, Exodus 4: 24-26, Joshua 7 and many more. The Christian's verdict on such passages is that they give a partial or distorted picture of the nature of God; and the reason for his verdict is what he knows to be the complete revelation of God in Jesus Christ, the Word made flesh.

We discovered, too, that the Old Testament had little or no thought of a life after death and that there were a number of passages (e.g. Ecclesiastes 3: 19; Psalm 88: 11-12) which emphatically denied that there was any real life beyond the grave. Christians repudiate the teaching of such passages and do so because Jesus has made it abundantly plain that they are in error.

We discovered also that, while it is mainly with regard to the Old Testament that Christians discriminate, sometimes they do it with the New Testament as well. The Christian refuses, for instance, to accept as a true conception of marriage that given in 1 Corinthians 7 which puts it on a level little higher than that of the beast. Again, the principle of discrimination is Jesus Christ, who has elevated the status of women and refined, enriched, and ennobled the relationship between the sexes.

In every instance considered of Christians discriminating in their use of the Bible, the principle of discrimination is Jesus Christ. This would strongly suggest that the key to the understanding of the Bible is Jesus himself, and the rest of the study we have made supports that conclusion.

In Chapter Three we saw that at many points Jesus dealt in discriminating fashion with the Bible. In passages such as are to be found in the Sermon on the Mount ("You have heard...but I say...") and in other places, he quite peremptorily corrected scripture – and the authority on which his discrimination was based was none other than his own. He patently considered that the teaching of the Old Testament was in error if it was at variance with his own knowledge of God and of his ways with men; and he

just as patently considered that he had the authority
to set it right.

We went on in Chapter Four to note that there
could be traced in the pages of the Bible the development of a number of ideas from a lower level to a
higher. By what standard does the Christian determine which is the lower and which is the higher end
of development in any given case? How is it that
without exception these ideas, according to the
Christian view, find their highest expression in the
New Testament? It is once again because of what has
been made known in Jesus Christ. In him is the
highest revealed and any development to be traced in
scripture must be a development towards him. And,
if it is found, as occasionally it is, that there is
development of an idea within the New Testament
itself, the standard of judgment is still Jesus. When
the Christian discovers, for instance that 1 Corinthians 7 gives one view of marriage and Ephesians 5
gives another, he regards the one as being lower and
the other as being higher according as he judges
them in harmony or in discord with the mind and
spirit of Jesus.

Surely, then, the key to the understanding of the
Bible is Jesus himself. We cannot accept all that the
Bible has to say undiscriminatingly as the Word of
God. Some parts of it are less so than others. The
principle of discrimination to be adopted towards the
Bible is the principle of the truth of God the Father
revealed in his Son. The Bible or any given part of it
speaks truly of God insofar as it speaks truly of Jesus;
and so any given part of the Bible may be reckoned to
be the Word of God to whatever extent it is in
harmony with the revelation of God in Jesus Christ.

This is the key we need. This is what will unlock the door to a proper understanding of the Bible.

Let me summarise the position at which we have arrived. We saw that it was impossible to regard the Bible as verbally inspired and that all attempts so to view it should be abandoned. We were forced to the conclusion that, even although the Biblical writers were moved to their writing by the Holy Spirit and were guided by that Holy Spirit in what they wrote, their writings were, in the last resort, their own writings, the products of their own minds, memories, knowledge and insight, and not necessarily free from error. This being so, the necessity became apparent to find some reliable method of determining when these various writers speak truly the message of God and when they do not. We believe that our required touchstone is to be found in Jesus and that Jesus, made known to us in the gospels, is the standard against which all scripture must be set, the bar to which all scripture must be brought for judgment, and the key to the Bible's message for our day. It is worth noting that this view is in perfect conformity with the opinion of the writer to the Hebrews when he said, "In many and various ways God spoke of old to our fathers by the prophets; but in these last days he has spoken to us by a Son" (Hebrews 1: 1-2).

6

DOES THE BIBLE SPEAK CREDIBLY TODAY?

If Jesus Christ is the key to the proper understanding of the Bible, it is obviously desperately important that we should know him well. It becomes, therefore, a matter of first importance that the picture of Jesus which the gospels give may be relied on with confidence. For the credibility of the Bible, the credibility of the gospels becomes crucial.

It should be borne in mind that the gospels neither claim nor endeavour to be full scale biographies of Jesus. They are selected memoirs, which unavoidably leave out a great many things that might well have been included. We find, for instance, that at one point in the gospel narrative Jesus says, "Woe to you, Chorazin! woe to you, Bethsaida! for if the mighty works done in you had been done in Tyre and Sidon, they would have repented long ago in sackcloth and ashes" (Matthew 11: 21, Luke 10: 13). But what mighty works were done in Chorazin we do not know for there is no other reference to the place in the gospel records.

Let me put it this way. The gospels give us not photographic records of Jesus that chronicle every detail but, what is really more valuable, portraits of him painted by reputable artists. They do not agree on every point but this is just what we should expect if the artists were men of competence and integrity. It would be strange if we found four painters each producing a portrait that was identical in every respect. Nevertheless, these four word pictures of Jesus drawn by Matthew, Mark, Luke and John are indisputably portraits of the same person and they make him unmistakably clear.

They do not agree on every point of detail, it is true, but neither do they disagree on any point of major consequence. What is more, when they are put together, they are seen to be so harmonious and the picture of Jesus that emerges from them so arresting as seems to make it self-evident that the gospels are authentic records.

This "internal evidence" might seem to many perfectly valid and sufficient reason for accepting the gospels' portrayal of Jesus as genuine and reliable. But it cannot be left at that. We must pursue the credibility of the gospels further. We have discarded the notion that the scriptures were dictated by God and so protected from all possibility of error. We must, therefore, assess the reliability of the gospels in the same fashion as we would assess the reliability of any other ancient documents. This being so, perhaps the best way to see how historically credible the gospels are is to trace the process that brought them into being.

That process began with the events with which the gospels deal, the events of Jesus' life, death and resurrection. But a number of years were to elapse before the gospels were written. Can we be sure that the memory of these events was accurately carried across the intervening space of time and that the task of recording them, when it came to be done, was executed with accuracy? These are the questions which confront us.

The process of transmission of the story of Jesus –
the passing it down from the time of the events to the
time that they were chronicled – began even before
the story had reached its final chapter, began even
while Jesus was still moving about Palestine, preaching his message and performing his works of mercy;
for already stories of his words and deeds were being
told and retold and some of them were being written
down. This state of affairs was an anticipation of
what was to take place during the decades between
the resurrection and the emergence of the gospels.

The period between the gospels and the actual
events which they record was one in which oral
tradition was the chief vehicle of the transmission of
the gospel story. "Tradition" means, literally, "something that is handed down"; and oral tradition means
something that is handed down by word of mouth.
Although, even from within the period of Jesus' own
lifetime, bits and pieces of his story were being set
down in writing, it was predominantly by means of
oral tradition that the story was preserved down the
years that separated the actual events from the
gospels. The things that Jesus had said and done, the
happenings of his life and death and resurrection,
were remembered and repeated, told and retold, week
after week, year after year, from the very beginning.

There were two main spheres in which the telling
and retelling of the stories of Jesus took place during
this period of oral tradition.

There was, for one, the meeting of his followers for
worship. Every time the Christians assembled together for this purpose, a large part of the service was
devoted to hearing someone of authority give reminiscences of the Lord.

There was, for the other, the preaching on the mission field. From the outset, the Christian Church was a missionary Church. Transformed and joyful as a result of Jesus' resurrection, the first Christians found themselves possessed of news so wonderful that they could not keep it to themselves. Consequently they used every opportunity to tell their stories of Jesus to all who would give them even a semblance of a hearing. This they did in Jerusalem to begin with and then increasingly further afield; and, wherever the early Christian missionary effort extended, its ruling concern and its unceasing practice were always to tell these stories over and over again.

So it was that in these intermediate years the Christians were continually repeating them, both to one another, in their conversations and in their worship, and to the unbelievers around them, in their evangelism and in their apologetics.

Most prominent among these stories and by far the most frequently told was the story of Jesus' death and resurrection. For this was the heart of the gospel, that Jesus who had been crucified had triumphed over the grave. One might say that this constituted the main stream in the river of oral tradition; but it was not the only stream.

Flowing parallel with it was the recollection of things that Jesus had said and done. It was important that these, too, should be remembered, for the corollary of having faith in Jesus the Saviour was that one must live in accordance with the example and the command of Christ the King. Thus it was that, all along, the reminiscences of Jesus that were kept fresh consisted of accounts not only of his death and resurrection but also of his deeds and his sayings.

E

Although in substantial correspondence, the form of the oral tradition as it existed in each Christian community would not be exactly the same. Each eye-witness would pass on a group of reminiscences that was not identical with what his fellow passed on; and the consequence was that, in time, each Church came to have its own distinctive list of favourite sayings and stories. Some stories would appeal to a certain community more than others, and these would come to be told more and more often, while others would drop gradually out of the picture.

It was in this way that the tradition of each community would be formed; and the result was that, while the main body of tradition was basically the same everywhere, no two districts were likely to possess exactly the same collection of reminiscences or reminiscences of the same incidents in exactly the same verbal form. The Church at Jerusalem, for instance, would contain in its tradition items that were absent from the tradition as possessed by the Church at Caesarea, and vice versa. In addition, some stories common to both traditions would be told differently in each. Soon these separate oral traditions began to assume stereotyped forms, as constant repetition rendered the respective groups of reminiscences more or less fixed in each Church and district; and so the oral tradition of each different area became a thing of individuality, basically the same as the rest but recognisably distinct from them.

It is of great importance to see clearly the situation I have been trying to describe. Perhaps I may be pardoned, therefore, for summarising what I have been saying. As soon as ever the Christian Church was launched by the tremendous happenings of

Easter and the following days, stories of Jesus began
to circulate freely on the lips of his followers, told
both for their own edification and for the conversion
of others. The apostles and other eye-witnesses were,
as by the very nature of the case they had to be, the
first narrators. Each selected such things for telling
as he reckoned most worth repeating and related
them in his own way. No two of them were exactly
alike either in their choice of reminiscences or in their
report of the same reminiscence. Consequently, right
at the beginning of the period of oral tradition, there
were issued, so to speak, different editions of the
memoirs of Jesus. They were basically the same as
one another but, nonetheless, quite distinct and they
provided the raw material out of which in time were
made the fairly rigid forms of the oral tradition that
came to be the property of the different Christian
Churches.

This might seem to suggest that reminiscences of
the various eye-witnesses formed separate entities in
the witness of the early Church and that they each
became eventually the fixed tradition of this branch
of the Church or that. That is not, however, what I
am trying to say. It was not a case of Peter and James
and John and the rest each coming out with his
"memoirs" of Jesus and issuing to the Church a
connected narrative. Their reminiscences were given
utterance mainly in the form of single stories and
sayings, or little groups of stories and sayings, as they
were called forth by the needs of preaching and
testifying, of counselling and exhorting.

The result was that in the first weeks of the
Christian Church there was given to it a great mass of
eye-witness accounts of things Jesus had said and

done, with special prominence being given to his
death and resurrection, and for a space these circulated as single anecdotes or sayings, or little groups of
them. When the Church spilled out of Jerusalem into
the surrounding country and out of Palestine into the
outside world, these personal recollections went too.
In every place where an outpost of the gospel was set
up, the central feature of its worship and its evangelism was the telling and retelling, much as they had
been first narrated, of some of the accredited stories
of Jesus.

At first in each Christian community the number
and nature of the reminiscences recounted would
follow no set pattern, except that everywhere the
passion narratives would be central. But, as time
wore on, each place would find certain stories more
attractive and more helpful than others and these
would come gradually to oust the others altogether in
the usage of that particular community until eventually that community had a fixed collection of "Jesus-
reminiscences" recounted in a fixed form. So it came
about, in process of time, that varying groupings of
the individual stories first told by the eye-witnesses
in Jerusalem and its environs were crystallised into
the set oral traditions of the various Churches.

As the years passed, the need began to be increasingly felt for the more important parts of the
gospel story to be enshrined permanently and
systematically in written form. This does not mean
that there was no writing down of any part of the
gospel story prior to the four gospels. The gospels are
the earliest written records that have survived, but
there were earlier writings than these, none of which,
unfortunately, is extant. In all likelihood, indeed, it

would be very early that people here and there would begin to write down some of their recollections of Jesus and it may well be that there was activity of this kind even before Jesus went to the Cross, perhaps in the shape of diary notes compiled by some of those who knew him intimately, such as Matthew whose business training would fit him well for this sort of activity.

One written document which, most scholars are confident, existed before the gospels is that to which they give the name "Q" (the initial letter of the German word "Quelle", meaning source). This was a very early document, probably going back almost to the time of Jesus himself and consisting mainly of sayings of the Lord, bound together by a thread of narrative.

That there were other writings, too, the opening veses of St. Luke's Gospel appear to make plain. As Moffatt translates them, these verses read: "Inasmuch as a number of writers have essayed to draw up a narrative of the established facts in our religion, exactly as these have been handed down to us by the original eye-witnesses who were in the service of the Gospel Message, and inasmuch as I have gone carefully over them all myself from the very beginning, I have decided, O Theophilus, to write them out in order for your excellency, to let you know the solid truth of what you have been taught" (Luke 1: 1-4). This is clear testimony to the existence of gospels before the gospels.

Nevertheless, for the first generation or so of the Christian Church there was comparatively little activity in the way of writing down the gospel tradition. It was only as the first generation of

Christians began to thin out and the voices of the
eye-witnesses, one after another, began to fall silent
that the need was felt to preserve the sacred story in
more definite and more enduring form. The canon-
ical gospels were the response to that need.

When this time arrived, those who accepted the
task of compiling written records found plenty of
material ready to hand, a mass of reminiscence
concerning Jesus which had been carefully preserved
down the years, some of it written but most of it in
oral form. The four Evangelists took this material,
both written and oral, examined and sifted it,
selected what seemed to each most worth recording,
and wrote the books which stand today at the
beginning of our New Testament.

The Gospel of Mark was the first to appear and, as
accurately as scholarship has been able to determine,
it was written between A.D. 60 and A.D. 65. The
foundation of this gospel is the memoirs of Peter, as
we are informed by Papias, friend of Polycarp who, in
turn, had been a disciple of the Apostle John.
Writing about the year A.D. 140, Papias says: ". . .
this also the presbyter used to say. Mark, who
became the interpreter of Peter, wrote accurately, as
far as he remembered them, the things said or done
by the Lord. But not, however, in order, for he had
neither heard the Lord nor been His personal
follower but at a later stage he had followed Peter."
This statement conjures up a picture of the young
John Mark accompanying Peter as he went about
preaching and teaching the gospel story; and of him
taking up his pen, after Peter was martyred, to write
down the story he had heard so often from the
apostle's lips. It may be, indeed, that he used

material which had come to him from Peter in written diary form and supplemented it from other sources.

Matthew came next and was probably published between A.D. 80 and A.D. 85. The title "According to Matthew" was prefaced in some later day to what was originally an anonymous work, and the gospel, as we have it, is not likely to have been written by the apostle. But the reason for its authorship being ascribed to St. Matthew may well have been that it was based upon, or grew out of, a diary kept by Matthew in which he recorded significant utterances of the Master. Papias, at any rate, tells us that Matthew was the author of such a document. He writes: "Matthew wrote down the sayings of Jesus in Hebrew and each interpreted them as best he could." It is by no means impossible that this early document of St. Matthew's is to be identified with Q. In addition to this primary source, "Matthew" made use of Mark and of other sources.

Luke was written about the same time as Matthew and has been described as the "most beautiful book in the world". Luke is the literary artist of the New Testament but, more important to us, he was also a careful and accurate historian. Modern scholarship and investigation have done much to substantiate his historical exactness and reliability. Luke drew upon many sources in the writing of his gospel, as its opening verses declare, including Mark.

The Gospel of *John* carries us into a different atmosphere. This difference was apparent from the beginning and a second-century writer, Clement of Alexandria, described it in these words: "John, perceiving that the bodily facts had been set forth in the gospels, being urged by his friends and inspired by the Spirit, composed a spiritual gospel." What he meant was that John, aware that the main facts were already well-known and widely circulated through the media of the other gospels, set himself primarily to elucidate the inner meaning of Jesus and his life and work. Assuming that his readers knew the story as told in the earlier gospels, John sought to supplement what these other gospels had already told and, at the same time, applied the fruits of a lifetime's contemplation to the interpretation for his readers of the inherent meaning of the facts. This gospel was written probably between A.D. 95 and A.D. 100 and, while John's authority seems to be behind the book, it is not likely to have been written by his hand. It is more likely that the actual author was one of the apostle's disciples and one who had been in close association with him for many years; and the probability is that he would gather his data partly from reminiscences written down by John, perhaps in the form of diary notes recorded soon after the events, and partly from sermons and informal talks given by him.

This brief outline of the process leading to the writing of the gospels might itself be sufficient to indicate that they must be substantially accurate transcriptions of the original. It may, however, be wise to amplify the argument a little by considering two questions that are often asked.

1. *Why was it so long after the events that the gospels were written?* It may seem strange that some 30 or 35 years should pass before the first gospel made its appearance, but there are several things to be

borne in mind:

(a) We cannot assume that nothing was put into written form before Mark came on the scene. As we have already noted, it is likely that several fragmentary accounts of Jesus' teaching and works were written in the pre-Mark period, although none of these, unfortunately, has survived independently. Some, however, would be used as sources by the Evangelists so that part of their content will be preserved in one or more of the four gospels.

(b) The Christians of the first generation believed that the end of the world was very near; and to them, consequently, the writing of books would seem largely irrelevant and unnecessary.

(c) Side by side with this was their intense missionary zeal and activity. They were so busy evangelizing the world that they had little time for sitting down and writing books.

(d) The main reason, however, was that during the first generation or so, there was felt neither need nor desire for written records. Books in that day were a comparative rarity and were expensive luxuries. Each copy of a book was, of course, an individual production, prepared entirely by hand, and a book corresponding to the size of the New Testament would cost a great deal of money. We are so accustomed to a constant flood of books from many printing presses that we find it difficult to visualise a time when books were scarce and difficult to acquire. But that was how it was in those far-off days, and books did not then enter into the everyday thinking of men as they do now.

More important still, the scarcity of books meant a greater reliance on memory work and oral teaching than we know today; and the Jews had been long accustomed to the practice of passing on their history and their religious and social teaching by word of mouth. One consequence was that the Jews counted the spoken word superior in authority and in value to the written word; and the early Christians, Jewish in origin and background, shared this prejudice and had it increased by their perfectly understandable feeling that it was much better to hear the stories of Jesus from the lips of someone who had been closely associated with the events than simply to read of them in a book or a pamphlet. So long, therefore, as there were still alive a number of people who had known the Lord in the flesh and could speak at first-hand of his life and death and resurrection, little room and little welcome existed for the more impersonal written record.

2. *Can we be confident that the tradition was perpetuated accurately through the period of oral tradition until it was finally set down in writing?* To twentieth-century Western minds it seems not unlikely that, since the transmission was so long a predominantly oral matter, the ultimate written form might deviate considerably from what was originally told. Again several things need to be kept in mind:

(a) The accuracy of verbal transmission on the part of the Jews was phenomenal. They mostly learned and taught by word of mouth. Their very word for instruction, *mishnah*, meaning literally, "repetition", suggests the learning by heart which was the actual custom. From the beginning they showed great natural aptitude for it and this, allied to long practice, produced memories of remarkable accuracy. This, indeed, was how it was in the East generally and many feats of memory were performed in the ordinary way of things, even by the very young, that would be a marvel in our modern Western world. For example, Nikeratos says (Xenophon: Banquet iii: 5), "My father, wishing me to grow up into a good man, made me learn all the lines of Homer; and now I can repeat the whole of the Iliad and the Odyssey from memory."

(b) The preservation of the tradition concerning Jesus was never a matter in which only a certain few were concerned. It was not a case of the tradition being looked after in secret by an exclusive little group and then, after a lapse of years, being made public and written down. From the beginning the tradition was the property of the whole Church and the whole Church was the guardian of its accuracy. We may be sure that, had any important deviation from the original ever been threatened, vociferous protest would immediately have ensured correction.

(c) Not only did every member of the Christian community have a part in maintaining the accuracy of the oral tradition, there were amongst that community actual eye-witnesses. This is a fact of great significance. Some people seem to assume that, after the initial telling of their story, all the eye-witnesses immediately and for ever withdrew from the scene. The fact is, however, that right up to the time the tradition was set down in writing,

there were eye-witnesses in the Church and their
oversight of the tradition in transmission must
have been more than sufficient to ensure its
substantial accuracy.

Let me try to illustrate. Most of us are familiar
with the party game in which a verbal message is
passed from one end of a line of people to the other.
The players are strung across the room, and the
starter whispers the message to the first person.
He, in turn, whispers the message – or what he
thinks he has understood it to be – to his neighbour, and so on down the line. At the end, the
message often arrives in a form grotesquely distorted from that in which it set out.

Some people seem to imagine it was like this
with the transmission of the gospel tradition. But it
was, in fact, considerably different. Imagine that
the room in which the game is played is one in
which people are coming and going continually.
At the beginning of the proceedings someone
narrates to the rest of the company events that he
and some companions, present with him in the
room at the moment, had witnessed only that
afternoon. Thereafter, the story is told and retold –
by the first narrator and by others – and, all the
while, there are arrivals and departures among the
company. This more closely resembles the circumstances under which the gospel tradition was
transmitted.

Imagine, further, that there are several rooms
with free passage between them, and that the same
story is told and retold in all of them, but started off
in each by a different eye-witness; and that, as the
evening wears on, more and more people begin to

write down parts of the story; and, finally, that at the evening's close four people who, if neither eye-witnesses nor present from the evening's start, have at least been present for some considerable time, write down in turn, with others assisting them, a systematic version of the story. Finally, these four versions of the incidents are passed round the whole company, amongst whom eye-witnesses still remain, and receive approval as substantially reliable reports.

This now gives a rough analogy of the process which carried the gospel tradition from the events themselves across some decades of mainly oral reminiscence and resulted finally in its being set down in the records that stand in the New Testament. The only reasonable conclusion is that with so many safeguards upon its accuracy, the tradition could not fail to be perpetuated with close fidelity to the original.

I make brief mention of two features of the gospel narratives which are further confirmation of their credibility.

(1) Some people are disquieted by the fact that the gospel narratives differ from one another at some points. The existence of such differences is, however, ground for confidence rather than mistrust. One would expect to find variation of detail between reliable, independent accounts of any set of events. No group of eye-witnesses will ever report the same incidents in exactly the same way and their reports will invariably contain differences on secondary points; but, if the witnesses are reliable, the reports will agree on the main facts. This is the kind of situation that the gospels provide.

It is true that they display differences on subsidiary points and occasionally on more substantial matters; but it would have been more disquieting if they had tallied exactly with each other on every item, as that would have provided grounds for suspecting a "tidying-up" of the stories to avoid any suggestion of disagreement. Their differences, so far from invalidating their testimony to the central facts, serve instead to confirm it.

(2) The credibility of the gospels is further corroborated by the presence in them of a number of features which cannot easily be explained otherwise.

There are certain things set down in the gospels which the Church could not have been very happy to see there and which only a strict honesty can have permitted to remain, sayings and references which were liable to be a source of embarrassment to the early Church and to cause difficulty or invite criticism. If in the process of transmission the tradition had suffered any serious modification, whether consciously or unconsciously brought about, these awkward items would certainly have been eliminated. Their presence in the gospel records demonstrates forcibly how conscientiously the Church, the custodian of the original eyewitness accounts, showed respect for the facts, even when the facts were uncongenial.

For instance, from an early period the Christians worshipped Jesus as God; yet we find it recorded that Jesus cried from the Cross, "My God, my God, why hast thou forsaken me?" (Mark 15: 34). Again, on not a few occasions, we find some reference to one or other of the disciples that shows him up in a bad light. The fact of such things having a place in the Early Church's official records cannot be explained unless these records have maintained a remarkable fidelity to the truth.

The Credibility of the Gospel Picture

There can be litte doubt that the gospel pictures of Jesus must be true to what he actually was and that each of them may be safely reckoned as giving a substantially accurate representation of what he said and did. Admittedly, no single one may be taken as one hundred per cent accurate but, even so, they need leave us in no doubt as to the true likeness of Jesus.

If you have four reputable painters each painting a portrait of a certain man, the portraits will have differences one from the other on points of emphasis and of detail. But they will be easily recognisable as portraits of the same person, and if you are unwilling to accept any one of them by itself as a sufficient guide to the subject's true likeness, all you need do is take the four portraits together. When these four homogeneous pictures are, as it were, superimposed one on top of the other and when there is left aside anything in any one portrait that may be in conflict with the testimony of the others, you will get a thoroughly reliable likeness of the man who was painted. It is just that kind of thoroughly credible picture that the four gospels provide of Jesus.

7

DOES THE BIBLE SPEAK RELEVANTLY TODAY?

Here, say, is a man speaking over the public address system at half-time during the cup final at Wembley Stadium. He is speaking in an unaffected, clear voice and can be plainly heard. He is using down-to-earth, immediate language and none of his hearers is in any doubt as to what he means. In addition, he is a man of known integrity. There is ample evidence that he is an authority on his subject and more than enough grounds, too, for accepting what he is saying as being true.

But scarcely any of his hearers are in the least interested in what he is saying because – audible, intelligible and credible as the message is – most of them find it not only quite irrelevant to their present situation but also an intrusion and an irritant. For the speaker is giving a potted history of the game of croquet and some hints on how to play it.

If the Bible is not relevant for modern man, it matters little or nothing whether or not it is trustworthy, whether or not it can be readily understood, whether or not it can be heard. Many people today do, in fact, reckon that the Bible is almost completely irrelevant.

The Bible has been subjected to many fierce attacks in its history; but it has survived them all. It is perhaps a parable of its durability that the house where Voltaire once lived, who said the Bible was finished, should have become the depot of a Bible Society.

None of the attacks made on the Bible is, however, as threatening as the attitude of the young man who just shrugs it off and says, "What can that book have of importance to say to me?" He is not interested in whether it is true or false, or a mixture of both. He is not caring whether or not the ethic it teaches is a practical possibility. He is not even indignant about its claims to deal in supernatural things. He simply refuses to allow any possibility that this book might have anything to say that could conceivably matter to his life in this age of space travel and planet exploration.

It is my belief that the Bible is no less relevant now than ever it was and by that I mean to say that it is very relevant indeed.

It is true that men travel through space in our day and the Bible knows nothing about space travel. But it is *men* who travel through space and the Bible knows a great deal about men and about human nature.

It is true that men have journeyed to the moon in our day and the Bible does not even begin to suspect that man would ever set foot there. But it is *men* who visit the moon and the Bible has much to say about the living of human life.

Human nature has the same basic needs as it has always had. Since the Bible's claim is that it speaks to these needs, it cannot, if credible, be dismissed as irrelevant. Anything but.

Just as, say, a cure for snake-bite is as relevant – if it works – to the twentieth century as to the first, so the message of the Bible – if reliable – must be as relevant today as in the beginning.

F

Everyone wants to make the most of his life. The Bible claims to have the secret of achieving this. It may, therefore, be written off as wrong, perhaps even as crazy, but scarcely as irrelevant.

The message that the Bible has to tell about Jesus of Nazareth – the message of his birth and death and resurrection, the message of the new life he makes possible for men – is called gospel because it is "good news" (which is what gospel means) and such good news can never be irrelevant.

This becomes all the plainer when we note that the Bible has a great deal to say that is pointedly concerned with twentieth century living.

The Bible is an old book admittedly but "old" does not necessarily mean "old-fashioned", and "old-fashioned" in any case need not mean "out-of-date". Time after time the Bible has things to say which are very pertinent to the circumstances and problems of man's way of life today.

Let us take some examples.

What theme is more topical or more relevant today than that of racial discrimination? The Bible has things to say concerning this. The burden of its message about Jesus makes it clear that in God's sight all men are equal, irrespective of colour or of race. One of the very things about Jesus that provoked hostility on the part of the authorities of Church and state was that he refused to be narrowly nationalistic.

A famous incident took place in Samaria, at Jacob's Well, near Sychar. This, incidentally, is one of the best authenticated of all Biblical sites. You can go there today and visit a well whose waters lie deep down in the earth and be sure that when you haul up the bucket from the depths and drink of its cool, clear water, that Jesus drank from this well too.

The story is narrated in the fourth chapter of St. John's Gospel. Jesus was making his way from Jerusalem to Galilee. The most direct route lay through Samaria – as it still is – but Jews travelling north to Galilee invariably took the longer way that skirted Samaria. The reason was the deep-seated animosity between the Jews and the Samaritans.

This animosity dated back to the period of the exile. During all the long years of the exile, the Jews, the people of Judea in the south, persistently refused to intermarry with their conquerors. They were determined at all costs to keep their race pure. But the people of the north, the Samaritans, were less rigid and a considerable amount of intermarriage took place.

When, with liberation, the Jews and the Samaritans re-occupied their territories and began to rebuild their way of life, the Jews ostracised their Samaritan brothers and neighbours because they had so badly, in their judgment, betrayed their race.

This hostility persisted to Jesus' day and it was for this reason that, if he could avoid it, no Jew would set foot in Samaria or have any dealings with a member of the Samaritan race.

Jesus, however, as the Bible narrative informs us, not only elected to pass through Samaritan territory for all the world as if Samaria were every bit as good to walk on as Judea or Galilee, he also chose to engage in a long and highly personal conversation with a Samaritan on the way, and a female Samaritan what is more, and a loose-living one at that.

All of which simply expressed once more what the words and actions of Jesus continually and consistently proclaimed, namely that all men and women matter, and matter equally, to God. It was a basic element of the message of Jesus that God does not discriminate in the least because of a person's race or colour. It was obviously implicit in this, and at other times it was explicitly stated, that Christians ought not to practise any racial discrimination either.

Paul puts it this way: "There is neither Jew nor Greek for you are all one in Christ Jesus" (Galatians 3: 28).

This is part of what the Bible talks about. What could be more relevant for our twentieth-century world with its racial tensions and its warfares of class, colour and ideology?

It is in the self-same sentence that Paul writes that, so far as Christianity is concerned, a woman is as good as a man. "There is neither male nor female; for you are all one in Christ Jesus." That is to say, the Bible declares, that there should be no such thing as discrimination on the score of sex. In an age when we hear and read much about Women's Liberation, who could suggest that the Bible is not relevant here?

Women's Liberation really came into being with the birth of Jesus. In the Graeco-Roman world of which Palestine was a small part when Jesus was born, most women had few rights, many had practically none and some had not even the right to live.

Jesus entered a world where the practice of "exposing" girl babies was not only common but was accepted without protest and apparently without any qualms of conscience. It was a nightly occurrence, for instance, to have a score or more newly-born baby girls laid out to die in the Forum of Rome. It was a regular early morning chore for the street cleaners to gather up their pathetic bodies. A much-quoted papyrus letter, found in the Egyptian sands early this century, illustrates the attitude of the time. A Roman soldier, on active service abroad, was writing home to his wife who was expecting a baby. In the course of chit-chat about a number of domestic matters, he refers almost casually to the coming child and says to his wife, "If it is a girl, put her out to die; if it is a boy, let him live."

If the baby is a girl, put her out to die! Not a dramatic, crisis-forced decision, not an exceptional circumstance, not something that society would count shocking. Just a calm, matter-of-fact state-ment about a course of action that no one would find surprising but which would be naturally and in-evitably adopted by anyone else in the same position.

The Bible tells of a Man who entered into this kind of world and affirmed that women, all women, also mattered to God. And that they should therefore, all of them, be respected by men too.

Jesus set forth these new standards both in word and in action. One day for instance, as we have seen, he entered into conversation at a well-head with a Samaritan woman – and talked to her at great length. Now, a Jewish Rabbi would not talk to any woman, even his own kin, out-of-doors, far less a Samaritan woman. In the Jewish world women were supremely important in the home. To the Greeks, women had no rights of their own. To the Romans, women remained in law children for ever. And even to the Jews, highly respected as women were in the home, they were things rather than people. A Jewish prayer ran: "I thank thee God that thou has not made me a Gentile, a slave or a woman."

Jesus, so the Bible tells us, had a different view of the matter. With his coming, the emancipation of womanhood began and this was the real beginning of Women's Liberation. Its real case and cause still rest in the kinds of things said and done by this Jesus. How then can we count the Bible anything but relevant here, whatever view we adopt of the issue itself?

What theme has greater relevance today than that of caring for others? What book has more pertinent things to say on this theme than the Bible?

There is, of course, that major Biblical theme, already touched upon, to which Jesus gave such clear and emphatic witness, that God is interested in all men and cares for everyone. He gave witness to this not only by what he said and by what he was, but also by the things he did and, not least, by the things which he allowed to be done to him. If God, then, has an interest in and concern for every individual whoever he might be, then those who would be godly men ought to be interested in and concerned about everybody else.

Jesus often spelled this out. Notably perhaps in the parable of the Good Samaritan. The stories Jesus told as parables were usually true-to-life affairs, things that had actually happened or could well have done. This was no exception.

The Jerusalem to Jericho road was notoriously infested by footpads and robbers. Travellers making that journey descended 3,600 feet in less than 20 miles. The road consequently dropped very steeply and took many turns. A multitude of corners, the

narrow defiles, the boulders offering ready conceal-
ment, made this road a paradise for brigands and it
well deserved the title "Road of Blood" often given it.
Even today when you motor down the new, straight
road, perhaps at 100 kph, even then you can readily
imagine how brigandry could thrive in such terrain.

This was the scene. Jesus told of a solitary traveller
making his way along this road when he was set upon
by thieves, assaulted and robbed, even stripped of his
clothes, and left lying at the roadside, more dead
than alive. He was still lying there when one of the
professional religious people, a priest of the Temple,
chanced to pass that way. He noticed the injured
man – he could scarcely have failed to do so – but for
reasons that seemed good to him, he hurried past on
the other side of the road.

He was scarcely out of sight round the next bend
when another churchman came by, a Levite, that is
to say one who assisted with the more routine tasks
involved in the Temple services. He, too, like the
priest before him, persuaded himself that he either
could not, or should not, lend a hand to the wounded
traveller.

These two men were followed by yet another
traveller on the way from Jerusalem to Jericho, a
Samaritan no less. Jesus being a Jew, his hearers
being Jews, and the Samaritans and Jews being
traditional enemies of long standing, the audience
would immediately assume that with the advent of
the Samaritan the real villain had appeared upon the
scene. In fact he turned out to be the hero.

Despite the inconvenience to himself, despite the
loss of time and the possible danger of exposing
himself to a robbers' attack (for the decoy method was

often used on that notorious road), the Samaritan halted at once to give what attention he could to the injured fellow lying at the side of the road. Not content with that, he put him on his donkey, took him to the inn which was the halfway post between Jerusalem and Jericho, and made provision for his further care there.

Jesus said to all who would listen then, and says to all who will listen now, that the Samaritan of the parable is the pattern of behaviour God expects. The needs of others are to be of first priority. Wherever we may give a helping hand to someone in need, whatever the circumstances and whatever the cost, it is our duty to do it.

The Bible reports Jesus as saying this kind of thing frequently, nowhere, perhaps, more plainly or more disconcertingly than in the course of that other parable which we usually call the Sheep and the Goats. There he says that the great test of whether a man has used his life well or not so well will be how he has used his opportunities of helping others. Your treatment of people in need is decisive. When you give or withhold assistance, you virtually give it to me or withhold it from me. "As you did it to one of the least of these my brethren, you did it to me."

This kind of teaching which the Bible attributes to Jesus has been the source and inspiration of present-day projects like Christian Aid and many others. I do not suppose that anyone would suggest that such matters are anything but acutely relevant to our day. How then can the Bible which inspired and still motivates them be classed as irrelevant?

Personal relationships are always a relevant issue because personal relationships are ultimately basic to all life. The Bible has a great deal to say in this field and some at least of the things it says may well be pertinent to community, national and international relationships as well.

There is that time, for instance, when the Bible reports Jesus as saying, "You have heard that it was said 'You shall love your neighbour and hate your enemy'. But I say to you, love your enemies" (Matthew 5: 43-4). The old standard was to repay evil with evil, with interest if possible. Jesus said he wanted his followers to practise love, even to those who did them injury.

He made this point quite vividly at times.

Once he said, "Do not resist one who is evil. But if anyone strikes you on the right cheek, turn to him the other also; and if anyone would sue you and take your coat, let him have your cloak as well; and if anyone forces you to go one mile, go with him two miles" (Matthew 5: 39-42).

Here are three illustrations, topical and typical, of the new standard Jesus was imposing on his followers.

When an injury was received or an injustice, there was to be no resentment and no retaliation. These illustrations are all dated now in a sense. But only in a sense. Their implications are as modern as when the words were first spoken.

"If anyone strikes you on the right cheek, turn to him the other also." It is significant that the *right* cheek is specified. If you, a right handed man as the majority of men are, stand facing another man and wish to strike him with your open hand on the right cheek, you can do so without contortion only with the back of your hand. The back-handed blow was, in Rabbinic law, the greatest of insults. Jesus is therefore saying that, even if you are subjected to the worst of insults, you should accept it with as good grace as possible and certainly ought not to retaliate.

The situation of slapping or being slapped as a calculated insult is not likely to be one in which many will be involved in our day and age. In that regard, the Bible is old-fashioned and irrelevant at this point. But insults have not gone out of fashion, more's the pity, and what is really being said here therefore is right up-to-date.

So with the other two illustrations. "If anyone would sue you and take your coat, let him have your cloak as well." The actual situation has been out-of-date for a long time; but the content of the illustration is anything but dated. A man's "coat" was his inner garment, a kind of long, loose-fitting shirt. Everyone, even the poorest, possessed at least two of these so that, if he lost one, he still had another left. The law said that a man could be sued for possession of his coat.

But the law also said that a man could not be sued for his "cloak". This was his large outer garment which he wore as a robe by day and used as a blanket by night. A man normally owned only one of these and the law gave him the right to hold on to this no matter what debts or liabilities he might have incurred.

Jesus says, however, that if a follower of his is sued for his coat, he should be prepared to let the suitor have his cloak as well.

What Jesus is really saying is that his followers should not make too much of their "rights". They should be more concerned with their responsibilities and with the needs of others.

"Coats" and "cloaks", as in the context here, have no place in our fashion scene, but the temptation remains for men to cling to their rights at the expense of more important things. When therefore the Bible says, as in effect it says here, that people are more important than rights, and personal relationships matter more than personal entitlements, you may conclude that its advice is not for you, but you ought not to accuse it of being outdated.

"If anyone forces you to go one mile, go with him two miles." The land which first heard the teaching of Jesus was occupied by a foreign power. The Romans had conquered Palestine and the Romans ruled it.

One of the laws of occupation was that any Roman soldier could conscript any Palestinian into service as a baggage carrier, up to the distance of one mile. This was accomplished by the soldier touching the civilian on the shoulder with the flat of his spear and telling him what he wanted him to do – and the civilian dare not refuse. This is what happened for instance to Simon of Cyrene who was conscripted in this fashion to carry the cross of Jesus to Golgotha.

Jesus says to his followers, "If this experience overtakes you, do what you are compelled to do and then offer to do as much again of your own free will."

The prerogative of a soldier of occupation to impress a civilian into baggage-carrying service is not itself a relevant issue in the world of today, nor likely ever to be so again. But the principle to which Jesus gave expression in this vivid way is every bit as topical now as it was then, for what he is saying is that his followers are not to be clock-watchers in the field of duty but ought always to be ready to go far beyond the limit of strict obligation in lending assistance to others.

There is no lack of other Bible themes which are topical in our twentieth-century world. "Freedom", for instance, is the watchword and slogan of great numbers today, especially of young people. The Bible declares that it knows the way to real freedom. It asserts that real freedom is not to be identified with total release from authority and rules. That would not be freedom but licence, and licence is really the worst kind of slavery. The Bible says it has the key to that true freedom which is freedom to do not what you want but what you ought. And this, paradoxically, is the acceptance of the seeming enslavement of the service of Jesus Christ:

> "Make me a captive, Lord
> And then I shall be free."

The Bible also deals, and very pointedly, with the subjects of love and sex and marriage. Not everyone in our day agrees with the Bible view of these things: chastity outside marriage, even the institution of marriage itself; but what the Bible has to say requires to be looked at and thought about before an attitude can legitimately be adopted or a judgment legitimately made.

There are many other instances where the Bible has pointed things to say about modern ethical and social questions. It could be argued indeed that there is no ethical or social question of today for which there is not a Biblical word.

The Bible, in fact, deals extensively and comprehensively with matters of human life – personal conduct, social matters, community relationships, international affairs. We may not agree with what it has to say. We may choose to reject its conclusions and its implications. But there are few, if any, fields of human behaviour where we can reach a defensible position without first taking into account what the Bible has to say and what down the years men have made of what it has to say.

The manner in which Biblical words and phrases (taken from the King James Version) have been incorporated into everyday speech may, it is true, prove no more than that the Bible *in the past* has been very influential. (I am thinking of phrases like "the skin of my teeth", "at the eleventh hour", and scores of others.) But it may also be a further indication that no judgment or decision to act is fully legitimate until and unless the Bible view has been taken into account.

Does the Bible have any relevance for today? That is the question before us. Many people think that space exploration is of little real relevance to the business of living. They are very much aware of man's voyages into space. They find space travel reasonably intelligible. They have no doubt about its credibility. They would not even withhold their admiration and their wonder.

But they are unconvinced about its relevance to the affairs of ordinary life. Many are like that with regard to the Bible in general and in particular to the message it has to convey concerning Jesus of Nazareth. It has nothing to say to them, they think, that has pertinence to the day-to-day business of living.

Most people, however, want to make the most and the best of their lives; and the Bible claims to hold the secret of how this may be achieved. We may choose, therefore, if we so wish, to write it off on other grounds but scarcely on the ground of irrelevance.

8

USING THE KEY

As we have seen, the picture of Jesus which the gospels present is the standard by which all other scripture must be judged; and also the key that unlocks the door to the essential truth it contains.

One obvious difficulty becomes apparent here and one very pointed question may be asked. It could be framed something like this: "If *all* scripture is to have its truth determined by reference to the picture given us of Jesus Christ, how can this test assess the accuracy or inaccuracy of Biblical reference to matters in the scientific realm? What help, for instance, does it give in deciding whether or not the Genesis story of creation is scientifically correct?"

The plain answer is that it does *not* determine the scientific accuracy of any of the Bible's statements and offers no help in deciding whether or not the story of creation, for example, is scientifically correct. But a plain answer is not enough. I must go on to say more.

It is vital to bear in mind that the Bible is a religious book first and foremost. It speaks primarily of God, of his nature, of his ways, of his will and of his purposes; but until it comes to speak of Jesus, it speaks often with a faltering, uncertain and, at times, mistaken voice. That is why we must take the clear picture of God given us in Jesus and view all the Bible in that light in order to uncover what it has to say.

That is, perhaps, reasonably simple. But in their compilation of the record, the various writers used –

could not avoid using, indeed – terms and categories
that were not specifically religious but were, it may be,
scientific or geographical. When, for example, the
opening chapters of Genesis seek to proclaim that God
is the creator of all things, they set that religious
message in a structure that is geological in character,
saying not only that God created but that he created
in such and such a way and in such and such an order.

When we apply our test to this, we find the gospel
picture of Jesus Christ confirming the message of
Genesis 1 and 2 that God is the creator. That is the
religious message and is what the writing is really
concerned to say. But what of the vestments with
which the message is clothed? What of the statement
it carries concerning the mode of creation? Our test
gives no help in determining whether this is accurate
or not and, in fact, is not in the least concerned with
that question. It is a religious test and gives a
corroboration of the religious message of the Genesis
story which is quite independent of the accuracy or
otherwise of its geological details.

From the religious standpoint, it is a matter of
irrelevance whether or not creation took place exactly as a literal interpretation of Genesis would suggest.
So far as the purpose of the Bible is concerned, what
it may say in terms of science and the rest is merely
incidental and secondary. It may well be extremely
important in itself, but the Bible's theme is God and
it is for knowledge of God that it is to be studied.

In that study the various parts of the Bible are to
be tested against the knowledge of God that we are
given in Jesus Christ; but non-religious matters that
may accompany the religious teaching are not assess-
able by reference to Christ. They must be judged by

reference to the fullest knowledge available in their
own field. That is to say, for example, that the truth
of the mode of creation is a matter for the geologists
and for geological research. The revelation of God in
Jesus indicates that he was able to create the universe, but it does not indicate how he actually did it.
The Bible is a text-book of religion; it is not, and does
not claim to be, a text-book of science.

Let me try to illustrate the point I have been
making. Suppose we are reading over the sermon of a
preacher of a past generation and suppose that he
employs a number of illustrations based on scientific
assumptions that modern learning has since shown
to be false. If we are asked to judge whether or not
that sermon is true, we do so, not on the basis of the
scientific "howlers" it contains, but on the basis of its
harmony or disharmony with our own knowledge of
Jesus Christ and the truth revealed in him. We do not
say, "This preacher is guilty of scientific error, therefore, all that he says is unreliable." Nor, on the other
hand, do we say, "This preacher speaks truth concerning Jesus Christ, therefore everything else he
says must be true, despite anything modern knowledge may have to say to the contrary." That is to
say, if we are wise we do not assume that the sermon
must either be true on *all* points or false on *all* points.

Let me simplify this illustration further. Suppose
this is one of the things said in that sermon: "The love
of Christ is so strong that nothing can break its hold.
As the atom cannot be split, neither can the love of
Christ be broken." Modern science, however, has
shown that the atom *can* be split. Do we then say,
"There is scientific error here, therefore the whole
statement must be false and the love of Christ cannot

be taken as the strong thing it is represented to be"? Or do we say, "There is religious truth here, therefore the whole statement must be true and modern science must be in error about having split the atom"? Of course we do neither of these things. We recognise that the preacher is concerned about a religious truth and about that alone, and that the scientific reference is purely incidental and secondary. Consequently we judge the validity of the religious message in the light of our knowledge of Christ and we judge the validity of the scientific assumption in the light of accredited modern knowledge; and we say, "What the preacher says is perfectly true, although his metaphor has been rendered obsolete."

To illustrate further, let me return to the creation story of Genesis. In brief, the Genesis narrative relates that God created the universe in a series of stages following one another in rapid succession. If then science were to show conclusively that the universe was not created in that way at all, it would make no difference to the religious message which the story is concerned to proclaim, viz. that "God created". When we bring the revelation in Christ to bear upon this religious message we find it not only confirmed but enriched, and its truth is independent of the scientific vehicle (or myth[1]) which conveys it.

This raises another point. So far as the Old Testament is concerned, too great an importance is commonly assigned to its facts *as facts*. While there is much of historical value in the Old Testament record, this aspect of it matters less than is often thought. The Old Testament depicts God's revelation of himself in history and man's apprehension of that revelation; and its witness to these things is largely independent of the accuracy of the facts it records. It is rather different when we come to the New Testament. With the gospels we have the record of the revelation itself and the facts here are of greater importance. For now we have the story of God assuming human flesh. It is no longer merely the story of God speaking through men and events, but the story of God-become-man directly and personally involved in events. The gospels are, therefore, by far the most important part of the Bible, the Old Testament being the story of the preparation for Christ and the rest of the New Testament being interpretation of him.

This last sentence indicates what makes the Bible, with all its diversity, a real unity. It is not a plateau but a mountain range of literature containing truth about God. Some parts of it stand nearer to heaven than others. The gospels tower far above all the rest and from their height it is given even to ordinary, unlearned folk to look down on all other scripture and assess how near it rises to God or how far away it drops.

When we look down like this from the Everest peak of the gospels upon the other books of the Bible, we see a definite pattern of development and advance. The earliest Old Testament writings form as it were the foothills and the later[2] books, broadly speaking, thrust up their peaks ever higher and higher. In other words, with some recessions here and there, each generation grasped a little more fully and a little more clearly the revelation God was seeking to impart, until in the fulness of time "the Word was made flesh and dwelt among us". With the coming of

Jesus, self-disclosure was complete. Now, for the first time, men were able to see fully and clearly what God was like. Now the summit was reached. All that went before were tokens and promises of this; and all that came after were attempts to view it in greater detail. It is in its testimony to Jesus Christ that this library of books which is the Bible acquires unity.

NOTES AND REFERENCES

1   *Myth:* Modern scholarship gives to the creation story – and to many more of the Old Testament stories – the name of "myth". This name is one whose very sound is enough to fill many devout hearts with horror; but we need not be so horror-stricken if we take time to grasp its meaning. "Myth" is really a technical term that is employed not to discredit a story but to describe the (unimportant) narrative form by means of which is conveyed an eternal truth. The ancient Eastern world was fond of using this method of teaching spiritual truths and we need not be surprised that many instances of it should be found in Old Testament writings – the stories of the Fall of Man and of the Tower of Babel are others that spring readily to mind. Still less need we be surprised when we remember that the limitations of our finite human understanding frequently compel us even today to act in like manner. We, too, find ourselves unable adequately to express God and the things of God and so we have recourse to "mythical" statements. If, for instance, we say to a child, "Jesus looks down on you continuously through the windows of heaven", we seek to convey the spiritual truth of Jesus' omnipresence by means of "myth"; or if we speak of Jesus "sitting at the right hand of God" we employ "myth" to express our belief in Jesus' unity with God.

When, therefore, the term "myth" is applied to one of the Bible stories it need not be taken as a term of disrepute. We are not thereby dismissing the story as a falsehood but are saying that we have here the expression of eternal truth in temporal categories. The story may or may not have a basis in historical fact, but that is not important. The important thing is the religious teaching it conveys.

2   We must remember that the books of the Bible do not stand in our canon in strict chronological order.

9

THE VALUE OF THE BIBLE

Some may regard the view of the Bible put forward in these pages as diminishing its value; but the reverse is the case.

It must be admitted that, on this view, the Bible can no longer be regarded as a repository of magical texts to which a man may turn for guidance on any and on every subject. No longer is it possible to take any text from here or from there and assume that its words, taken in isolation, are the absolute words of God and the instruction of God for whatever situation confronts us. In every instance we must be prepared to dig much deeper and to scrutinise each text in the light, not only of its actual words, but also of its context and of its period, and, above all, of the gospel picture of Jesus Christ. This may, indeed, seem to some to lessen the Bible's authority, to restrict its scope and to weaken its helpfulness for Christian faith and life. In fact, it leads to an increase of the Bible's authority, a widening of its scope and an enhancement of its helpfulness for Christian faith and life. Its value is made greater not less.

To regard the Bible as "word for word God-given" has the effect of discrediting it and rendering much of it irrelevant for modern minds and modern needs. But when we come to see the Bible as the record of a religious development culminating in God's supreme self-disclosure in Jesus, the position is radically

altered. None of it now is without relevance and
potential value to the serious seeker. Even the lowest
levels touched by its authors, even the grossest errors
of which they are guilty and even the most striking
imperfections that they display, when lighted up by
our knowledge of Jesus, may all have something
worth while to say concerning our Christian faith
and conduct.

The reason is this. The Bible speaks not only of
God but of men; it deals not only with God's revelation of himself to man but with man's progressive
apprehension of that revelation. In doing so, it has
much to say of man's foolishness and sin, of his
frequent culpable failure to grasp the revelation as he
might and as he ought, and of his repeated shameful
spurning of the path along which it beckons him. The
consequence is that, no matter what spiritual stage a
man may have reached, there is invariably some part
of the Bible that exactly mirrors his position and his
need; and, conversely, we may take almost any part
of the Bible and be confident that it reflects
someone's present situation and present problem.

This is in marked conflict with the verbal inspiration view which is compelled to insist that every part
of scripture stands firmly on its own feet and contains
a message from God quite independent of its place in
any "progressive revelation" and quite recognisable
apart from any reference to the rest of the record or
even to Jesus Christ. Those who support this position
believe that it makes the whole Bible authoritative
for faith and conduct, and that our view weakens, if it
does not altogether destroy, the Bible's authority.

It is true that our view does not permit us to assign
equal authority to all parts of the Bible, for we have

come to see that the Bible contains different levels of
authority. *The* authority is Jesus, presented to us in
the gospels. These are, therefore, the supremely
authoritative part of the Bible and the rest of the
Bible has authority to the extent that it is corroborated or illumined by Jesus. While this means
abandonment of the notion that the Bible has a
uniform authority, it leads at the same time to an
extension of its real authority.

For now we are enabled to focus on the true
ground of the Bible's authority which is Jesus Christ.
The verbal inspiration viewpoint tends to obscure
this because of its insistence that from Genesis to
Revelation the Bible speaks with unanimous voice of
Christian things. The indisputable fact is that it does
not and the consequence for the authority and use of
the Bible is disastrous. What happens in practice is
that much of the Bible is simply left out of account by
the Christian who tries to adhere to this position.

Freed from the fetters which this viewpoint im-
poses, we are better able to recognise that true
authority resides not in the mere words of scripture
but in the Christ to whom the Bible testifies. To him
we are to take our problems, from him we are to seek
guidance, by him we are to be commanded how to
live. This does not mean that, apart from the gospels,
the Bible is depreciated in value. The reverse is true.
The other parts are, in a sense, less binding on us and
less important than the gospels; but at the same time
their proper function is uncovered and their true
value brought to light. They help us to understand
Christ, his teaching and his mission and so cause us
to realise more fully the authority he lays upon us. No
longer tempted to make the Bible a collection of

magical texts, we are compelled to refer all things to
Jesus Christ and to acknowledge his authority in
every situation.

We do not, of course, receive from Christ explicit
instructions for every circumstance. Most frequently
we have ourselves to interpret his will for the circumstance of the moment. It must be admitted that there
is danger in this, the danger that a man may be
imperfect in his understanding of Christ or that he
may be influenced too much by his own bias or
prejudice. But this danger exists even on the fundamentalist view and it is one that can never entirely be
evaded.

The Pharisees, for instance, thought they could
escape this kind of danger by codifying the will of
God into a set of regulatons which would cover every
conceivable situation. Their attempt was an impossible and largely a profitless task, as such an attempt
must always be. Jesus does not legislate for every
individual situation but gives eternal principles
which are applicable to all circumstances.

There is real danger that an individual's interpretation of Christ's way may go astray; but the more
thoroughly he gets to know Christ, the less likely this
becomes. If, then, the Bible is to assume its highest
value, we must recognise not only that Jesus is the
key to the scriptures but also that we need to know
him as fully as possible. To do this, we must carefully
study the gospels, the only written records we possess
of Jesus' life and work.

This study will be greatly aided if we do not rest
content with reading the Authorised Version but
make use, in addition, both of modern translations
and of modern commentaries. The Authorised

Version has gained a place in the hearts of the English-speaking peoples that is unrivalled by any other book or any other translation. Nevertheless, modern translations are always a great aid to understanding. It is a pity that there is still to be found suspicion of any rendering of the scriptures into modern language. Some would almost seem to count it sacrilege to make a new translation of the Bible, repeating, perhaps, the attitude of the young American deacon who objected to the Revised Version on the grounds that "if the Authorised Version was good enough for St. Paul it was good enough for him."[1]

The English-speaking peoples have had the Authorised Version for so long that it is difficult sometimes not to think of it as the original itself. But we ought never to forget that the Authorised Version is not only itself a translation but was, of course, a *modern* translation when it first came out in 1611. It owed its origin to the desire to give the Bible to the people in their own language so that they could read it for themselves with understanding. After more than 370 years that language is no longer quite the language of the people. The coinage of words is continually being new minted and some of those in the Authorised Version are either not any more in regular currency or have changed their value. The language of the Authorised Version, beautiful though it often is, at many points is not clear to the modern reader and at some points is difficult if not actually misleading. If, then, we wish to learn of Jesus to the fullest possible extent, we ought to read the gospels not only in the Authorised Version but also in a modern translation.

Nor ought we to be content to read the gospels
with no aid to understanding other than the printed
text. These books were written about nineteen centuries ago and, while their perennial freshness and
astonishing clarity are among the marks of their
uniqueness, the fact remains that we miss something
of what they have to say and teach if we ignore the
help that the scholars have to give. Much valuable
information is available on matters like the background of the country and people in the time of Jesus,
geography, customs, dress, meaning of words and so
on. To avail ourselves of this is to have the gospel
picture of Jesus filled out for us; to refuse it is to
impoverish our understanding of him and his
mission and message.

I have been laying such emphasis on the importance of the gospels that a question must have arisen
in many minds, namely: "What place is left for the
rest of the Bible?" If the gospels matter so very
much, must not the remainder of the Biblical writings, by comparison, occupy a decidedly subordinate place?

That is a correct reading of the situation. We are in
error if we attempt to set all of the Bible on the one
plane as being itself the revelation of God. The Bible
is not the revelation of God but the record of God's
revelation. That is why the gospels should not simply
be set alongside the rest of the Bible as if they were
simply part of a whole. The gospels belong to a
category of their own for they are the record of the full
and perfect revelation of God given in Jesus. They
are unique and by far the most important documents
that the world contains. All other writings, even in
the Bible, are subordinate to them.

This is not to say that the other books of the Bible are lacking in importance. They have great value, but it needs to be rightly understood.

Following the gospels in importance comes the rest of the New Testament, especially the epistles of Paul. These writings are early attempts to elucidate more fully the meaning of Jesus for human life and, since they were written by men who either had known Jesus in the flesh or were saturated in his Spirit as well as in the Church's teaching about him, their importance is considerable. Admittedly, they cannot be taken to be infallible interpretations of Jesus at every point, but they are of great assistance to those who desire to know him better.

The Old Testament writings are less important but they, too, have considerable value. They are the record of that progressive grasp of God's revelation by the Jews which served as a[2] preparation for the advent of Jesus. This being so, the Old Testament scriptures can assist us to a deeper understanding of Jesus and his teaching and work. But to do so they must be read in the light of the gospels and read with an understanding mind. The Old Testament is not for casual reading. It is not a book for the beginner in spiritual things; it is a book for the mature Christian.

NOTES AND REFERENCES

1   J. P. Smyth, *How we got our Bible*, p. 44.
2   *a:* I say "a" preparation, rather than "the" preparation because it is not possible to imagine – and Paul corroborates this view – that God was seeking to reveal himself only to the Jews. He must have been seeking to reveal himself to all nations. The people of Israel, however, were the most responsive to that revelation and so it came about that it was in the historical context of Jewry that God worked out his plan of salvation and sent his Son into human flesh.

10

THE TRUTH OF THE BIBLE

Associated with the general question of the Bible's credibility is the particular question with which we have, indeed, already been skirmishing: "Are some parts of scripture just not true?" To this question the reply must undoubtedly be given that, if truth is to be measured in terms of strict factual accuracy, then some parts of the Bible, particularly in the Old Testament, are not true. To leave our reply there, however, would not itself be strictly truthful as it would give a false impression. Much more needs to be said.

To begin with, we must ask, like Pilate, "What is truth?"; but, unlike Pilate, we must stay for an answer. Truth is rarely a matter simply and solely of strict factual accuracy. If a child should say that a certain distance is "miles and miles", we do not reckon him to be telling an untruth even although the actual distance is no more than 880 yards. The child's description of the distance, although not factually accurate, is a correct description of how far it appears to him. Only a pedant would say that his answer is false. Similarly, if another child should speak of God dwelling in "a castle in the sky", we may smile but we do not term his statement a falsehood. The fact is that both these children are speaking the truth *as they see it*, and, while that may be a long way short of the real truth as we know it, we recognise a partial truth in what they say.

This is by way of introduction to the argument of the present chapter and to it I add this observation. Children frequently speak of God and of Jesus in the most human terms. The familiarities and the anthropomorphisms which they employ would be counted gross and shameful in an adult; but in the mouths of children they have a winsome charm and at times may even seem to bring us nearer to reality than many a more accurate statement has been able to do. They are not the full truth. They are often very far away from the full truth, often absurdly far away, and sometimes little more than a caricature of it. Yet something of the truth belongs to them. They are not rightly termed untrue and not infrequently they may even be helpful to those who are in possession of the full truth.

When compared with the full revelation of God in Christ – the "judging" of scripture discussed earlier – the Old Testament is seen to reflect the spiritual childhood which was the forerunner of Christ's coming and the preparation for it. In some parts it will be found to be more childish (that is, less advanced) than in others; and in some parts it will be found to display surprising maturity and closely to anticipate what lies ahead. When judged in this way, the Old Testament will clearly be seen to fall short of the full truth made known in Christ, sometimes very far short, sometimes even shockingly and shamefully short. But that is not necessarily the same thing as being untrue. It may be only partial truth, it may be a distortion of the truth but, if it contains even a glimmering of truth, it is not competent to write it off as "false".

This gives an indication of how we ought to think of the Bible's truth. It would not be correct to say categorically that the Bible is wholly true; nor would it be correct to state boldly that certain parts of the Bible are false and may be discarded. In a real sense – in the most real sense, indeed, since the Bible is a religious book and its major concern is religious truth – there is little, if anything, in the Bible that can properly be classed as untrue and thrown aside. At the same time, there are many things in the Bible which come short of the full truth. There are passages in the Bible which, it must be recognised, are "spiritually childish". These, however, are mostly to be reckoned not as "untrue" but as portraying some eternal truth of God in partial or erroneous form. It is in this way, I believe, that the "truth" of the Bible must be viewed and I pursue this line of argument not for the sake of creating a Bible apologetic which will conserve the Bible's value and relevance to the maximum degree – although, incidentally, it does this – but simply because that is how it is.

I cite one or two examples which may drive my argument home. The regulations concerning the offering of sacrifice occupy a large and important place in the Mosaic Law. Christians rightly pay no practical heed to these, for Jesus has rendered them obsolete by revealing how inadequate it is to make such offerings to God and how imperfect is the view of God that thinks that this is what he wants. But this does not mean that the "sacrificial" parts of the Bible are false. Rather, they record a fragmentary and anticipatory grasp of the truth – eventually to be made fully known in Jesus – that God demands of his worshippers the best they have to give.

We may note, for instance, how anxious the regulations are to ensure that no imperfect animal shall be given in sacrifice. It is to be "without blemish". Implicit in this – no matter how dimly or mistakenly understood – is the truth which later men of God were to apprehend more clearly (cf. Micah 6: 8) and which is so fundamental to the teaching of Jesus, that only our best is the offering to lay on the altar of God. The Old Testament sacrificial system construed that in terms of material things. Jesus has shown that God demands it in terms of a spiritual offering – of our love, our loyalty and our service – but the beginnings of the truth, nevertheless, are to be detected in these Old Testament passages. The perfect revelation of God in Jesus Christ shows for the first time how far short of the full truth they come and yet shows for the first time also the real truth in them.

Another example is provided by the Old Testament injunction to exact a life for a life – e.g. Exodus 21: 23-25: "If any harm follows, then you shall give life for life, eye for eye, tooth for tooth, hand for hand, foot for foot, burn for burn, wound for wound, stripe for stripe." This ethic of retribution has been completely outmoded by the Christ who said, "Do not resist one who is evil", and "Love your enemies". It may seem that Christ's words show the Old Testament at this point to be utterly false without any redeeming feature at all. But, again, we have here an embryonic truth about God which the revelation in Jesus both judges and makes plain.

In the earliest stage that the Old Testament reveals it was regarded as proper that, when a wrong was done, unlimited vengeance should be exacted. The upshot of this was that one injury done – a killing, say – led to an interminable sequence of others. The "life for life, eye for eye, tooth for tooth" commandment meant a restriction of this practice. It was a limiting of the act of vengeance to the equivalent of the original injury and while still, when viewed against the background of Christ, a primitive and savage kind of morality, it was more merciful than the morality it superseded. It was a step towards the mercy that was God's real desire, an anticipation, even though faint and far off, of the royal law of love which ultimately Jesus was to enunciate in all its fulness. Despite its initial appearance to the contrary, the Old Testament is seen in this instance, too, to be not wholly false, although partial and imperfect in its apprehension of the truth.

Another example is found in Deuteronomy 20: 16-18, where we read: "But in the cities of these peoples that the Lord your God gives you for an inheritance, you shall save alive nothing that breathes, but you shall utterly destroy them, the Hittites and the Amorites, the Canaanites and the Perizzites, the Hivites and the Jebusites, as the Lord your God has commanded; that they may not teach you to do according to all their abominable practices which they have done in the service of their gods, and so to sin against the Lord your God." Here is a command that the Israelites should ruthlessly exterminate the inhabitants of the territory they are about to occupy as their own – and the command is represented as the wish of God. It is obvious that God as we know him in Jesus Christ could never have ordered the Israelites to act with such merciless cruelty. We ought not, however, to conclude that these verses are totally untrue. Although they are a gross distortion of the truth, something of the truth is in them.

Once again, the Israelites had laid only imperfect hold on what God was trying to say to them. They felt – and rightly felt – that they were under obligation to keep their religion pure and themselves free from any taint of heathenism. Accordingly, they felt it was their God-given duty to exterminate all the heathen in their vicinity – for how else were they to keep their faith and worship untainted? We know now, through knowing Christ, that they were terribly wrong in their idea of the means God wished them to employ for the preservation of their religious purity. Nevertheless, the idea expressed in this and similar Old Testament passages was not wholly wrong. However distorted, there is truth there that is still valid for us; for we, too, must seek in God's name to abolish the heathens – not, however, by killing them but by making them Christians.

These illustrations, which are typical, may be sufficient to show that the Old Testament is not to be regarded as false either in whole or in part. Our view of the Bible does not deny truth to the Old Testament, far from it, although it does insist that its truth may not lie so much on the surface as some suppose; it does not entail casting the Old Testament overboard, far from it, although it does mean that it is given its proper place, not side by side with the gospels but subservient to them; it does not render the words of the Old Testament valueless for the Christian, far from it, although it does require that these words should be interpreted in the light of Christ's revelation, by which their real truth, as well as their imperfection, is made plain.

It may be well to amplify a little what I mean when I say that the truth of the Old Testament is not

H

always "lying on the surface". To be sure, my meaning may well have been made sufficiently clear by what I have already said in this chapter; but it may be wise all the same to recall what I said earlier about the Bible being essentially a *religious* book, with a supremely religious theme and purpose. To forget this is to run the risk of going astray in our understanding of it.

This could happen, for instance, with the story of the Fall of Man (Genesis 3). If we begin to concern ourselves unduly with the incidental elements in this story we are likely to miss the religious message it is intended to proclaim. If, that is to say, we count it a matter of first importance to determine whether Adam and Eve ever existed as individual historical personalities; or to determine where, if at all, the Garden of Eden is to be located as a geographical situation; or to determine whether the serpent actually spoke with a human voice; then we are missing the point of the passage.

This passage, like the rest of the Bible, does not have an anthropological purpose. Its function is to teach something religious – in this particular instance something concerning the nature of man. It is this essential religious message that matters and the other elements in the story are a mere feathering of the arrow for flight. Their factual accuracy or inaccuracy in no way affects the real truth of the narrative and should not be permitted to blind us to it.

If we leave out of account the factuality of the accompanying details or even reject it, the real truth of the story is unimpaired. The story tells – as the gospel tells and as our own experience confirms – that

man is a fallen creature in need of salvation, a sinful
being in need of redemption, a rebel against God in
need of reconciliation.

The truth of any part of the Old Testament cannot
be fairly estimated unless these things be borne in
mind: that the question at issue is one of religious
truth; that we shall often have to dig beneath the
surface for the truth a particular passage contains;
that the more we know of the background and context the better chance we shall have of unearthing
that truth; that we must first learn what the passage
did say (i.e., what the original writer intended to
convey to the original readers) before we can hope to
learn what it *does* say (i.e., its abiding message to all
generations); that only rarely will the Old Testament
be found to enshrine any gospel truth in fully-
developed form and that both what it lacks and what
it possesses of real truth will ultimately be seen only
by reference to Jesus Christ and the revelation of God
given in him.

Before closing the chapter, I refer back once more
to the expression I used that not always did the truth
of an Old Testament passage "lie on the surface". By
this I meant that often its real significance was to be
detected only by digging beneath or behind its actual
meaning. I believe that I have made plain the
intention behind my use of the phrase but it may not
have been altogether the happiest of choices. Others
have spoken in somewhat similar terms of Old Testament truth and yet have meant something vastly
different. There have been those in the course of the
Bible's history who have maintained not simply that
the real *truth* of an Old Testament passage was often
to be found underlying its meaning but that its real

meaning often underlay its surface, or apparent, meaning. These are they who have adopted the allegorical[1] method of interpreting the Old Testament.

This is a method of scriptural interpretation that goes back to the Rabbis. The position confronting them was this. On the one hand, a number of the regulations which stood in the Law, both moral and ceremonial, belonged to earlier and more primitive conditions than now obtained and were no longer able to be observed. On the other hand, these regulations were part of Holy Scripture, and Holy Scripture, they believed, was literally the Word of God. Obviously God would never have allowed anything to be written in scripture which was not wholly true nor even anything which might grow irrelevant or have to be regarded as unimportant. How, then, was this contradiction to be reconciled? They found their answer in an allegorical treatment of scripture.

God, they declared, often did not mean just what he literally said in the scriptures. His words frequently had a hidden meaning and this hidden meaning the Rabbis "elucidated". Their "elucidation", however, was often no more than a reading into the scriptures of their own preconceived ideas and a forcing of them to mean simply what they wanted them to mean – a characteristic which has tended to accompany every use of the allegorical method. It was due to this allegorical method of approach that, for instance, the Song of Songs achieved a place in the canon of Old Testament scripture. This book is a lyric of human love and not a specifically religious book at all. As a result, it was not at first accepted into the canon. But the Rabbis allegorised it as a song dealing with the love existing between God and Israel and so eventually, on the basis of this interpretation, it won its way into the Hebrew Bible.

The Rabbinic method of allegorising the Old Testament has been widely used by Christians as well. Faced with the same fundamental difficulty as had confronted the Rabbis – a difficulty, moreover, greatly aggravated for them by the truth of God revealed in Christ – they have attempted to find a solution along the same lines. The literal meaning of many an Old Testament passage was obviously either not absolutely true or not applicable and yet, having been (as they thought) rigidly controlled by the Holy Spirit, every passage must possess absolute truth and absolute relevance, and so recourse was made to allegory.

H. E. Fosdick[2] speaks at length of Origen's use of allegory as an illustration of how this method has been employed by Christians of many generations to accommodate the Old Testament to the idea of its inerrancy under God.

Origen, writing at the beginning of the third century, recognised clearly that the Old Testament contained many features of thought and of morals which were patently far outgrown and quite impossible to defend as God's revelation. The first chapters of Genesis, for instance, seemed to him ridiculous if taken literally; the Old Testament anthropomorphisms often shocked him – references such as to God having hands and feet, and to his being angry and repenting were, to his mind, blasphemous if taken literally; many details carefully narrated in the Old Testament, such as the furnishing of the tabernacle, he considered too trivial, if taken at their face value, to be the voice of God. In allegory he thought to find relief of the problem. "Unworthy ideas of God, inapplicable laws, outgrown customs, and patent contradictions were all read away by means of the mystic sense. The letter was but the body of a passage; the allegorical interpretation was the soul."[3]

In the early Church and in the Church of the Middle Ages allegory was regularly employed in this fashion and has been similarly employed, although to a diminishing extent, down to modern times. Still in the present day there are those who would seek to preserve the theory of a verbally inspired Old Testament by allegorising its apparently obscure, irrelevant, outgrown, or un-Christlike sections. This, however, is a method of Biblical interpretation that is unjustifiable.

It never was justifiable but, if possible, it is even less so now that it was in Origen's day. For now we know, with a certainty that ought to admit no doubt, that the words of scripture have only one proper sense and that is their original sense. For this certainty we are indebted more to John Calvin, perhaps, than to any other. Calvin condemned out of hand the allegorical method and insisted that the native meaning of the words of the Bible was their only meaning.

But, while they were staunch upholders of this principle in theory, the reformers fell, in practice, into an error similar to that of the allegorical approach which they so forcibly denounced. They did not possess adequate instruments of historical knowledge and research and, as a result, while they believed that they were always interpreting the scriptures literally and bringing out the original meanings, they frequently read meanings into them that did not really belong. They often practised, as H. E. Fosdick puts it, "eisegesis" in the name of "exegesis", and so, in the event, handled the Old Testament in a fashion not greatly dissimilar to the Rabbis. It was in this way, for instance, that Luther could say, on the one hand, "To allegorise is to juggle with Scripture"; and could say, on the other hand of Psalm 3: 5 ("I lie down and sleep; I wake again, for the Lord sustains me"), "Christ, by the words of this verse, signifies his death and burial, for it is not to be supposed that he would have spoken so importantly concerning mere natural rest and sleep."

In some such manner as this advocates of the verbal inspiration theory of scripture have sometimes tried to make defence of the inerrancy of the Old Testament. But the way to meet the facts of the case – that many parts of the Old Testament are outmoded in their portrayal of God, in their interpretation of God's will, in their use of outworn categories – is surely not to attempt to bolster up a verbal inspiration theory by artificial means. It is to accept these facts; to recognise that the Old Testament records man's developing apprehension of the revelation which God was always seeking to impart; to uncover the original connotation of its words; and, then, courageously and expectantly, to seek out their abiding truth by reference to Jesus Christ, who is the key to the understanding of all the Bible.

NOTES AND REFERENCES

1   *Allegory:* An allegory is a story or statement in which every detail is intended to convey a second meaning over and above its obvious or apparent meaning; and it is this second or inner meaning which is the whole point and purpose of the allegory. The best-known example of allegory in English literature is John Bunyan's *Pilgrim's Progress* where every person, every event and every detail stand for someone or something else.
2   H. E. Fosdick, *The Modern Use of the Bible.*
3   Ibid. p. 76.

11

HOW TO LISTEN TO THE BIBLE

I have tried to show that the Bible does speak today and that what it says is both credible and intelligible. What it has to say is of supreme importance both with regard to the life to come and with the day-to-day business of life here and now. It is, therefore, vital that we should learn to listen well to it.

This entails, to begin with, that we remember the nature of the Bible. Although we call it *the* Bible, it is in fact a library of books, sixty-six of them, written at different times, by different writers, in different styles, even in different languages and written, too, with different aims and purposes.

At the same time it is justifiably called *the* Book, because there is a thread that binds all its pages together and that thread is its witness to God. For all of the Biblical books deal in some way or another with the nature of God and his dealings with mankind.

Not that they give a uniform witness. The Bible contains widely differing levels of testimony to God and sometimes the differences are very marked. That is to say, the Biblical writers were not always accurate in the witness they bore. God was always eager to make himself known but man for his part was able to grasp that revelation only little by little, and sometimes quite erroneously, until Jesus came and revealed God in a human life.

The gospels are our written record of this supreme revelation and the picture of Jesus they present is the key that unlocks the door to a thorough grasp of the meaning and value of all the Bible. If then we are to let the Bible be properly heard, we must first study the gospels and get to know them as well as we can.

Another thing to remember, as we engage in the exercise of letting the Bible's voice be heard, is that the Bible does not claim to be an authority on every subject under the sun. It is the world's most important book. But it is a *religious* book, concerned to tell the story of God's dealings with men and of the way of life he has provided for them through faith. This is its theme; and its purpose is the salvation of men.

In pursuing this purpose, the Bible often has remarkably fine things to say and some remarkably accurate information to offer in other fields. But its subject is God and it is highly dangerous to try to make it a text-book of science or geology or anything other than religion.

I suppose the Bible might be roughly likened to the Highway Code. The Highway Code does not tell us how to grow turnips or how to run a jumble sale; but it gives information essential for making a proper use of the roads. Similarly, the Bible is not an authority on all subjects but it gives information essential for making a proper journey along the road of life, not authoritative on all matters but indispensable for the job in hand, that of living life well and of getting safe home at journey's end.

Psalm 119: 105 sums it up:

> "Thy word is a lamp to my feet
> and a light to my path."

Here is a picture of a man making his way through a dark and uncertain place with a lantern to guide him. Now, a lantern is not the sun, making everything clear. A lantern lights up the immediate area, and shows the traveller where to put his feet, helping him to avoid the pitfalls and enabling him to find his way.

We must, however, be prepared to work at letting the Bible speak to us. In many ways it is not an easy book. All its writings are old and little of their background is readily known to us. To get the maximum benefit from the Bible requires us to devote time and effort to studying it, using modern translations and up-to-date commentaries.

It is important, too, to read the Bible with some kind of system. It is far from being the best approach just to begin at Genesis and to read right through to Revelation.

Nor is it advisable simply to read the Bible haphazardly, simply opening it at random and reading what we meet. I like that story of the man who thought he could find instant guidance by using that method. Faced with some kind of problem, he decided to "let the Bible speak". He decided to let his Bible fall open and to accept as God's word for him whatever his eye lit upon first. But the first words he caught sight of were, "Judas went and hanged himself".

Not finding this very much apparent help, he tried again. This time he read, "Go and do likewise". By now thoroughly put out, he permitted himself a final try. This time he came up with the words, "that thou doest, do quickly".

It is important to have some systematic method of Bible reading. We may work something out for ourselves or we may adopt one of the many such plans which are already available; but it is most advisable to be systematic.

Some, I know, will reckon that the view of the Bible put forward in these pages means a demotion from the position it occupied on the verbal inspiration view. In my opinion, however, it enhances rather than decreases its value and importance. I have already indicated my reasons for that opinion (see chapter 9).

There is, however, one other point sometimes made in this connection that we may consider. The verbal inspiration supporters commonly maintain that my view of the Bible is bound to lessen its effectiveness as an instrument of evangelism. They contend that demonstrably the most effective preaching is "genuine Bible preaching", by which they mean preaching based on a verbal inspiration view. In support of this contention, attention is drawn to notably successful evangelical campaigns of the past and present. "Here is what happens," it is said, "when you get real Bible preaching. It is when the preacher accepts the Bible as wholly the words of God that the Holy Spirit finds its fullest release. The verbal inspiration view of the Bible works. What more need by said?"

Much more need be said. The view of the Bible I have been putting forward undoubtedly is much different from that of the fundamentalist with his verbal inspiration idea. It represents the Bible's uniqueness as consisting not in how it was written but in what it has to say; it represents the Biblical writings as being not all of equal consequence but as containing different levels of value, with the gospels mattering most and the rest subsidiary to them; it represents these writings as not all bearing the same witness to God but displaying a developing grasp of him leading up to his complete self-revelation in Jesus; and it represents the words of the Bible not as identical with the words of God but as containing the "Word of God" to an extent that must always be assessed by reference to Jesus.

I believe this is the view of the Bible which the facts of the case demand. If this, then, is the correct view, the question of whether or not the verbal inspiration approach makes for a more effective instrument in the hands of the evangelist does not come into it; in fact, however, I do not believe that it does.

No one would deny that there have been many and wonderful results from this so-called "Bible preaching"; souls have been saved and lives have been changed to an extent which it is impossible to measure but the echo of which will surely reverberate through all the corridors of time. This is an occasion for heartfelt thanksgiving to God – but it does not prove the fundamentalist's point.

How can we tell whether or not the preacher, in any given instance, might have accomplished even more if his preaching had been based not on the verbal inspiration view of the Bible but on the other? The circumstance that his "Bible preaching" brought results does not at all prove that his attitude to the Bible was correct.

We need to be careful of our logic here. We have two facts before us. A man preaches on the assumption that the Bible is composed of the "words of God"; and God blesses that preaching richly. It does not necessarily follow that God blesses that preaching *because* of the Bible-attitude on which it is based. It is just as legitimate (and, in the light of our previous findings, a great deal more justifiable) to infer that God blesses the preaching *in spite of* it.

God often has used, does use, and no doubt, will continue to use, imperfect agencies for the advancement of his kingdom; and the fact that a man's preaching has brought results is no proof in itself that his view of the Bible is the most effective for preaching purposes. After all, farmers were able to raise crops, and frequently very good crops, before as much was known as is known today about the science of agriculture; but we would scarcely suggest on that account that farmers ought to continue to employ the old methods even when they conflict with the requirements of modern knowledge. Surely the farmer's skill and care will produce even better results when freed from the shackles of past ignorance and allied to the fuller understanding of the present. Similarly, if the fundamentalist preacher were to take his attributes of sincerity and of enthusiasm, and his gifts of eloquence and of personality, and were to ally them to a sounder view of the Bible, is it not likely that the results accruing would be of even greater value for the kingdom of Christ? God must surely make more effective employment of truth than of error or of half-truth.

During the nineteen centuries and more that the Christian Church has been in existence, many wonderful things have been accomplished by the grace of God. No one would suggest that these things are proof that the Church has been absolutely correct in her doctrine all that time. Such has clearly not been the case. The Church has laboured under many

errors of thought during that period, sometimes under
what are now apparent as gross errors; and often the
wonders of God have been performed not because of
right doctrine in the Church but in spite of wrong
doctrine. The fact that God can and does work within
the context of a given situation does not necessarily
mean that everything in that situation is true and best.
God was at work even in the darkest days of the
pre-Reformation Church in Europe. Even then some
were finding their way into new life through the grace
of the Lord Jesus Christ. Such happenings, all would
agree, were not so much due to the prevailing situation as in spite of it; and with the Reformation there
came a liberation of the Holy Spirit which indicated
how greatly the errors of the medieval Church had
been hindering the workings of God.

I believe that the Holy Spirit would be further
liberated and God would be able to work even more
freely, if Christians universally adopted the attitude
to the Bible put forward in this book.

This conviction has been reinforced by my own
experience. As a boy, I thought of the Bible as the
inerrant words of God and continued so to think of it
when I became a Christian. I began, however, to be
increasingly disquieted by its difficulties and
apparent contradictions and errors. I kept pushing
these aside for a while, but they left me uneasy. In my
more honest moments, I had to admit to myself that
the reason for my anxiety was fear that, after all, my
faith might rest on an insecure foundation and that
the book on which my faith depended might turn out
to be fallible. Then I came to see another view of the
Bible – the one outlined here – and with the acceptance of this, it was as if I passed from the limited

security of the inner harbour of literalism out into the more demanding but more rewarding waters of the open sea, with my priceless chartbook daily explained by the Supreme Pilot. The Bible was a greater help to me from then on and my faith became much more solidly based. No longer did I fear for its security. For now I recognised that my faith was not dependent on the infallibility of a Book but rested on the trustworthiness of the Saviour to whom the Book gave witness.